BIBLICAL LEADERSHIP

D1452754

BIBLICAL LEADERSHIP

Developing Church Volunteers

KENNETH O. GANGEL

EVANGELICAL TRAINING ASSOCIATION
PO Box 327, Wheaton, IL 60189

All Scripture quotations, unless otherwise indicated, are taken from The HOLY BIBLE, NEW INTERNATIONAL VERSION®. Copyright © 1973, 1978, 1984 by International Bible Society. Used by permission of Zondervan Publishing House. All rights reserved. The "NIV" and "New International Version" trademarks are registered in the United States Patent and Trademark Office by International Bible Society. Use of either trademark requires the permission of International Bible Society.

Scripture quotations marked (ESV) are from The Holy Bible, English Standard Version, copyright © 2001 by Crossway Books, a publishing ministry of Good News Publishers. Used by permission. All rights reserved.

Scripture quotations marked (NKJV) are taken from the New King James Version. Copyright © 1979, 1980, 1982 by Thomas Nelson, Inc. Used by permission. All rights reserved.

Cover Design: David LaPlaca debest design co.

Produced with the assistance of The Livingstone Corporation (www. LivingstoneCorp.com). Project staff includes Linda Taylor, Cheryl Dunlop, Joel Bartlett, Kirk Luttrell.

ISBN: 978-1-929852-80-2

TABLE OF CONTENTS

PREFACE

North Americans have not only learned to live with an "edifice complex," we have clasped it to our collective bosoms as the final answer to "reaching the lost" in the 21st century. Buildings. Bigger buildings. More elaborate buildings. These buildings, of course, depend on money. When we encounter a problem in the church we develop a plan to throw some more money at it, assuming it will be solved. Trouble with the teens? Hire a new youth director. Janitorial service not up to par? Let's forget this volunteer idea and hire a professional firm.

How typically cultural all this seems! How like the secular leaders of our time have we become! And how alien to the Scriptures are these impersonal ideas of entrusting the progress of the faith to paid employees and bigger buildings. Does it work? Many times it does. The whole concept behind pragmatism is whether something does what it is intended to do. But the larger question remains: Is it biblical?

The New Testament puts behind it the Old Covenant trappings of kings, warriors, holy battles, elaborate temples, and bloated budgets. How simply, yet clearly the Good Shepherd speaks of His sheep, how they must be fed, tended, guarded. How person-centered the ministry of Paul who pours his life into Timothy, Titus, Luke, Epaphroditus, and so many more. The money? It goes back to Jerusalem to help with famine relief.

Of course we need trained and adequately paid "clergy" by whatever name we call them. But the genius of the New Testament church rests in lay leadership, all God's people equipped for ministry. That is what ETA stands for, and that is what this book is all about. May the power of Christ, through the Holy Spirit, design your life to answer His call to use your gifts in the service of the King.

My thanks to Karen Miller for typing the manuscript and to Jennifer Jezek at ETA and others at the Livingstone Corporation for long, tedious hours of editing these pages.

This book is dedicated to my four grandchildren—Lyndsey and Bradley Gangel and Madison and Philip Gardner—already leaders in their own worlds and future leaders of the Church.

Kenneth O. Gangel

ACCEPTING AND APPLYING BIBLICAL LEADERSHIP

"We have different gifts according to the grace given us. . . .
If it is leadership, let him govern diligently." (Rom. 12:6, 8)

I

Biblical theology rests at the foundation of our understanding of Christian leadership. I do not think that leadership is a subset of the social sciences—like psychology and sociology—with its main task being how to deal with people. We can learn a lot from those fields, but for the Christian, leadership is a biblical and theological issue, and that's the way we will approach it.

Three Problems in Grasping Biblical Leadership

We face several problems in doing it that way. First is the *American success syndrome* that is very obvious in our day. In most elections every candidate points to himself or herself as a really good and honest person who could lead the country or a state. Meanwhile the candidate points to other people as indecent, incompetent people for whom no one should vote.

Americans are committed to successful people. Think of all the television programs that flaunt celebrity this and celebrity that or lifestyles of the rich and famous in one form or another. The American success syndrome—measuring success by how much money or influence one has—is one of the great horrors of our time, and it stands in the way of a biblical understanding of leadership. The Bible's description of leadership is not at all like the modern world's understanding of success, especially in the Western Hemisphere.

The second problem is *infatuation with size.* Have you ever asked yourself, "Can spiritual formation be measured quantitatively? Do we really disciple people in expectation that they will pray more times a week than they did before, or read more Bible verses? If they increase their Bible reading from twenty-five to fifty verses a week, is that spiritual formation?" The Bible doesn't say so. Scripture measures spirituality qualitatively. Is a denomination better because it has more churches than other denominations? I doubt it. History has shown us that large denominations can go bad theologically despite their size or prominence.

Finally, we fight the *compulsion to imitate*. Remember, there is no one model of leadership. There is no New Testament precedent for franchised ministry. Consider the distinctions between Jerusalem and Antioch, two completely different churches, yet both very effective in their own ways. Jerusalem dominated its own country, and Antioch was a sending church, the mother of many churches. We really face only one bottom-line question here, and you'll read it numerous times in this book: *Why has God raised up this church or ministry, in this place, at this time, and what does He want from us?* Do we look like the mega-church around the corner? Do we look like the ministry of the month? Wrong questions!

Learning Biblical Leadership

As we study leadership in the Old Testament we do not find didactic passages that say, "Leaders do this; leaders do that." So we use character studies or models and look at figures such as Joseph, Moses, David, Joshua, Solomon, Nehemiah, and dozens of others.

We look at both the positive and the negative behaviors. For example, David was a marvelous king but a terrible father, and God wants us to see that. While David was off killing Philistines, his kids were killing each other at home. We don't learn fatherhood from David; we learn leadership as a warrior and a leader of men. We dare not miss the reality of these lessons.

In the New Testament we see a change from an Old Covenant to a New Covenant model, and all Christian leaders must grasp it. Many people lead and teach leadership from an Old Covenant model based on prophets, priests, and kings. That explains why some ministry leaders behave like kings. "This is my ministry; I'm in charge; I do what I want with the budget; I do what I want with the programs." This reflects an Old Covenant model of leadership. The New Covenant, the New Testament, calls us to a new model of leadership, and it offers many didactic lessons. It shows us the difference between people being chained together and forced to behave a certain way and people who serve of their own free will.

Jesus used New Covenant techniques in training the Twelve. I hope you have had a chance to read A. B. Bruce's book *The Training of the Twelve*, in which he argues that Jesus did not spend most of His time with large crowds, nor did He spend it with individuals.[1] As much as we like to think of discipleship as being a one-on-one relationship, Jesus spent most of His time with small groups. As a leader you will develop small groups of potential leaders and work with them.

Sometimes it seems like a slow learning curve to move from Old Covenant to New Covenant leadership. When you get discouraged with the way people respond, just read through Mark 9. See the six major mistakes that the disciples made in forty-eight hours. The disciples! Hand-picked learners of Jesus Christ! And they were fairly well along in their seminary training. Yet they made mistake after mistake. They just did not get it. Why? Because they were Old Covenant people.

They didn't catch on until the book of Acts, when the Holy Spirit filled them. As the book of Acts opens, what was their biggest question? "Okay, it's been great, the miracles, the parables, the resurrection; everything was terrific. But now is it time to restore the kingdom to Israel?" All they could think of was their political agenda! Jesus said, "It is not for you to know the times or the seasons—the Father keeps that hidden; that's His business. Your job is to communicate the Gospel to the world and leave the rest to God." So don't worry about being a slow learner in leadership; and please be patient with others who are also slow learners. That will be essential if you want to be an effective biblical leader.

Contemporary Cultural Corruptions of Biblical Leadership

Second Corinthians 10:1–5 reminds us that the weapons with which we fight are not the weapons of the world. Have you ever seen leaders try to fight with the weapons of the world? Have you ever watched them try to schedule agenda items at a time most favorable to them? Have you seen them manipulate meetings so they get their own way? Such behavior breaks my heart because it defies the principles of leadership that the Lord emphasized for His disciples.

We have swallowed the idea that *money provides the answer for everything.* If we need more workers in the church, we "buy them." The country works that way; states work that way; so do churches. But the New Testament does not give that impression at all.

Then we face *the prosperity gospel factor*—the idea that those in the Lord's work will wear alligator shoes and drive Cadillacs. Few ministry views are more contrary to the teaching of the New Testament. This is one of the worst cultic heresies of our time—that God demonstrates His blessing by material prosperity. Actually, we find the converse of that in the New Testament, where Paul says, "I glory in only one thing—my suffering" (see 2 Cor. 11:30). Certainly we thank God when we are able to buy a new car after we've driven an old junker. God's grace made it possible. But that is not the only way He shows His blessing. He might "bless you" by giving you the flu for three weeks, a chance to rest, pray, think, and be grateful for good health when you have it again.

Assertiveness, taught in many Christian leadership books, is another cultural corruption. Assertiveness plagued some of Jesus' disciples. He taught them self-control, being careful what one says, and keeping one's mouth shut at the appropriate time. Yes, there may be times when biblical leaders must be assertive (e.g., Jesus at the temple in John 2), but our problems usually come from too much self-promotion, not too little.

Political clout is our fourth problem, the idea that either extreme, left or right, could control the country. This is Americana. This is the cultural "stuff" of our day, described by Ron Enroth in *Churches That Abuse*[2] as control-oriented leadership, isolationist attitudes, spiritual elitism, lifestyle rigidity, discouragement of dissent, and a painful exit. Keep in mind that Enroth is writing about the cults. Discerning Christians recognize that this list describes almost any cult. What is disturbing is that we find many of these problems in evangelical churches. Not all of them, and maybe not to the extent that they appear in the cults, but we see these things in the lives of too many Christian leaders.

Some Key Passages

Take a look at Matthew 11 and 12. Here Jesus talks to His disciples and reminds them that if they come to Him they will find peace of mind, and their weariness will be dispelled by rest. "Come to me, all you who are weary and burdened, and I will give you rest. Take my yoke upon you and learn from me, for I am gentle and humble in heart, and you will find rest for your souls. For my yoke is easy and my burden is light" (Matt. 11:28–30).

This passage divides neatly into three parts: first, the *invitation* to Christlike leadership. Who should come? Weary leaders and burdened leaders. Second, we see the *qualifications* for Christlike leadership: gentleness and humility. You will read often about that in this book. And finally, the *education* for Christlike leadership: learn to take the yoke, learn to share the burden.

Learning to take the yoke means that biblical leaders have certain responsibilities; they serve in a "yoke." So often when we see this verse we think only of the old analogy of the double yoke of oxen with Jesus in one side and the Christian in the other. That describes a good way to handle the issues and problems of life. But Jesus is also trying to teach the disciples leadership, and the issue at stake is enormous. Learn to take the yoke, the responsibility. "Yes, I am a Sunday school superintendent. Yes, I am the pastor of this church. Yes, I am a women's ministry leader. I will take the yoke." But learn to share the burden; that's what this course is about: team leadership.

Learn to share the burden. You do not do it alone. Not one Jesus and one disciple, but one Jesus and twelve disciples. And when one failed, Jesus replaced him with another. Leadership is team ministry. We see only one place in the book of Acts where Paul ministered on his own without the ministry team around him—Acts 17, in Athens. And that was not a planned ministry opportunity. No need to suggest Paul did wrong; he was so stirred up he could not hold himself back (a common reaction for him), so he just spoke out and jumped into the Mars Hill controversy. But every other time he ministered with a team around him, and that teaches us a very important lesson.

Here is another crucial passage.

> *Aware of this, Jesus withdrew from that place. Many followed him, and he healed all their sick, warning them not to tell who he was. This was to fulfill what was spoken through the prophet Isaiah: "Here is my servant whom I have chosen, the one I love, in whom I delight; I will put my Spirit on him, and he will proclaim justice to the nations. He will not quarrel or cry out; no one will hear his voice in the streets. A bruised reed he will not break, and a smoldering wick he will not snuff out, till he leads justice to victory. In his name the nations will put their hope." (Matt. 12:15–21)*

This is a prophecy of the Messiah, but also a great description of biblical leaders. Do you know leaders who quarrel? Do you know leaders who cry out, shout, call attention to themselves? Do you know leaders who march up and down the streets complaining about this or boycotting that? Do you know leaders who would rather get rid of weak and struggling people in the church than try to heal them?

Master this tremendous lesson: *Restraint characterizes biblical leadership.* Not power, not volume, not visibility, but restraint. How often we think that leaders who talk the loudest, or have the most political clout, or maybe the most money, or the most piercing eyes, are the leaders God has chosen. Samuel discovered the foolishness of such thinking in his task of anointing David as king. Remember Barnabas and the wonderful qualities of that servant? Consider how the Bible describes his humility and willingness to encourage other people as the trademark of his leadership.

What Biblical Leadership Is Not

In Luke 22, we read Jesus' words of instruction to His disciples at the Last Supper. Does this sound like the familiar politics you know?

> *Jesus said to them, "The kings of the Gentiles lord it over them; and those who exercise authority over them call themselves Benefactors. But you are not to be like that. Instead, the greatest among you*

*should be like the youngest, and the one who rules like the one who
serves. For who is greater, the one who is at the table or the one who
serves?" (vv. 25–27a)*

Logic tells us it is the guest at the table; but that would be wrong. Jesus
said, "I am among you as one who serves" (v. 27b), hence the term "servant
leadership."

New Testament leadership is not authoritarian attitude: not having
power over other people; not being able to tell other people what to do; not
controlling other people.

New Testament leadership is not political power play: not manipulating a
vote in a business meeting; not interfering with the nominating committee
to get the people you want on the ballot; not using the threat of resignation
to get your way. Never use the technique of the kings of the Gentiles.

New Testament leadership is not cultic control: not the power of
personality or position. This is not about theological cults, but the power of
personality—personal dominance. The great example here, as ugly as it may
seem, is Adolph Hitler. Historians can find no logical reason from Hitler's
experience, background, and education why he should have become the
leader of Germany. But the power of his personality dominated thousands.
They were mesmerized when they heard him speak in those big beer halls.
Eventually, the man threatened the world.

Let's Get Positive!

We had three negative lessons; now we look at three positive lessons.
New Testament leadership is nurture. In 1 Thessalonians 2:7, Paul uses the
wonderful image of a nursing mother to describe his and his companions'
leadership. He writes, "We were gentle among you, like a mother caring for
her little children." We picture here a mother bird on a nest, spreading her
wings over the baby birds, taking care of them, making sure the rain doesn't
hurt them, making sure the cold wind doesn't blow on them. This sounds a
lot like "a bruised reed he will not break."

New Testament leadership is example. Perhaps we should call it *modeling.*
We find this later in the second chapter of 1 Thessalonians when Paul says,
"You are witnesses, and so is God, of how holy, righteous and blameless
we were among you who believed" (v. 10). In essence, Paul is saying, "You
know what we were like when we were among you; you remember how we
behaved; you saw what we did. We're asking you to behave that way as well."

New Testament leadership is fatherhood. If you check my website (www.
morninglightministries.com), you'll find a book I wrote with my son, called

Fathering Like the Father. We focused on the transferable attributes of God and showed how human fathers can replicate them in human fathering. That is the analogy Paul uses here in 1 Thessalonians. He reminds the church there that he and his companions dealt with each of them as a "father deals with his own children, encouraging, comforting, and urging" them to live worthy lives (vv. 11–12). Christian leaders are models like mothers and fathers. They care about little things like cold, wind, and rain on the "little birds." And they care about security, about taking care of the family, about protecting people.

Getting Down to Reality

We need to make a switch here for a moment from looking at biblical texts to developing some understanding of what biblical leadership looks like. Leadership can focus on the leader's traits, abilities, personality, experience, training, and credentials, but *leadership cannot be defined by looking at the leader alone.* For years, experts believed it could. I earned my Ph.D. at the University of Missouri in the 1960s, and we were taught the leader is everything. But the Bible does not view it that way. And now forty years of research has led secular experts to debunk this old view.

Leadership must also focus on the group. Leadership assists toward mutually agreed-upon goals. What folly exists, for example, in asking a pastoral candidate to outline a vision for a church. The candidate has probably come to town for the first time, and he has come to the church for the first time. The search committee says to him, "If you come as our pastor, what would be your vision for our church?" He cannot answer that question! If he tries to answer it, he will simply explain what he has done at his previous church, which might not at all be what God wants to do in this church. The only right answer to that question is, "Friends, I just got here; please, you tell me what your vision is for your church." *Why has God raised up this church or ministry, in this place, at this time, and what does He want from us?*

And then, *leadership is always situational.* Ethics are *not* situational; morality is *not* situational; but leadership is always situational. Just because one can lead in one situation does not mean she will be a leader in another situation. An effective leader in a rural congregation may not be a good leader in an urban situation. Just because one is a good teacher does not mean he will be a good superintendent. Leadership situations differ greatly. We all do some things well, and we know we have leadership capabilities in those areas. But there are things we do not do well, and we should look for anonymity when those situations come along.

Traditional Leadership Styles

Traditional styles fall into three very general categories. The first is *autocratic leadership*—the military model, the need-to-know basis. Everything is approved by the boss or the superior officer. "Yes sir; no sir; of course, sir." This works well with children. You don't sit down and have a dialogue with a two-year-old approaching a hot stove or walking out into a busy street. You say, "Stop!" That sounds very autocratic.

This also appears often in church planting. Church planters rarely have people around them who know what to do, so they call the shots. Recognize that there are times when you use autocratic leadership, when it's necessary. But as the church grows, you don't hold on to that. You parcel out those pieces of authority; you empower other people. If after five years you're still running everything, then you have a leadership problem.

The opposite of autocratic leadership is *free rein leadership*. (Never put a "g" in this word when you write it; it completely changes the meaning.) Free rein means just letting the reins go, a common academic model. I have been a dean in two different schools, including years at Dallas Seminary. I can tell you that one cannot use autocratic leadership with eighty Ph.D's, half of whom hold tenure. One cannot lead as an autocratic leader; one must lead with a free rein. And if you can't lead free rein in that situation, you are likely to fail.

The third category would be *team leadership*. Decentralization is the key here. Decentralization means moving things away from the center, pushing things down from the top. You decentralize everything: decision-making, authority, the solving of problems. Problems should be solved as close to the line of fire as possible. For example, no Sunday school teacher should make a decision that a student or an assistant teacher could make. No superintendent should make a decision that a teacher could make. No Christian education director should make a decision that a superintendent could make. No pastor should make a decision a Christian education director could make. That's decentralization. Too many ministries are far too centralized, holding power in a small group of people or even in one person; and in my opinion that is unbiblical leadership. Think of these three styles as a continuum with autocratic on the right, free rein on the left, and team leadership (participatory) in the middle.

One thing is clear here; all leaders must know their styles, and they must understand how leadership takes place in a given situation. We call this "intentional selection of leadership style." Sadly, too few Christian leaders have an intentional selection of leadership style. They just do what comes naturally; they do what they saw their pastors or elders do; or maybe they act upon whatever they read in a book. What's your primary leadership style—autocratic, free rein, or team leadership? You may have come upon it accidentally or may have deliberately cultivated it. The Instructor's Guide that accompanies this textbook (available from ETA) will aid you in analyzing your own leadership style.

Wrap-Up

Now we need to put all this together. Your intentional leadership style should not be Old Covenant. You are not a king. You are not (in the Old Testament sense) a prophet. You are not a priest. You do not have charge of a nation. You do not have charge of the church. You do not have control over the ministry. You are God's servant. You are the Matthew 11, Matthew 12, Luke 22, 1 Thessalonians 2 person. You are a New Covenant leader. You lead *by restraining yourself, not by overpowering other people.* You lead by being a biblical leader, and you want God to help you produce other New Covenant leaders. You dare not be a dominant person, bossing everybody else, telling them what to do, pushing your own agenda, but hurting people in the process—and then expect people you are training to be humble, loving, gentle leaders like Jesus Christ who take the yoke and share the burden.

For some of you this may be a huge change. It certainly is for many of my D.Min. students. They say, "I can't believe this; I've been a pastor for sixteen years and no one has talked to me like this about leadership before. All I've heard is 'change agentry' and 'taking charge' and 'running the church' and being a 'mover and shaker.'" My friends, those are cultural terms and they represent a cultural leadership.

Biblical leadership takes prayer, self-discipline, and years of learning. It requires disciplined Bible study. But by the end of this course on leadership you should be able to put together the skills to be a New Covenant leader in the biblical model.

Remember the motto we have repeated several times already. *Why has God raised up this church or ministry, in this place, at this time, and what does He want from us?* We might even make that more personal by asking, Why has God made me a leader at this time and in this place, and what does He want from me?

Digging Deeper

1. What other New Testament passages relate to biblical leadership?

2. Give examples of unbiblical leadership attitudes or practices in the church today. What do you see as the most pressing problem/s in church leadership?

3. Have you intentionally chosen a leadership style? If so, is it autocratic, free rein, or team leadership?

4. Who or what do you consider to have been the greatest influence on your leadership style?

5. How have you experienced situational leadership?

Notes

[1] Alexander B. Bruce, *The Training of the Twelve* (Grand Rapids, Kregel Publications, 1971).

[2] Ron Enroth, *Churches That Abuse* (Grand Rapids: Zondervan, 1992).

Paying Attention
to Administration

"And in the church God has appointed . . .
those with gifts of administration." (1 Cor. 12:28)

2

We face three problems in talking about administration in the church or in Christian organizations. One is when people tell us that it is *just not essential*; another is when people tell us it is *just not interesting*; but the worst is when people tell us it is *just not spiritual.* But then we look at the Scriptures and we see people like Joseph and Nehemiah exercising the principles of administration, and in the New Testament, James at the church in Jerusalem in Acts 15 serves as a great example.

We must always remember that *leadership* is not the same as *administration.* Administration and management are identical terms, but leadership is different. However, there is hardly any type of ministry in which you don't do both. In Washington there must be hundreds, maybe thousands of people who are administrators but who exercise no leadership whatsoever. Then think of a quarterback on a football team, clearly the leader, but with no administrative responsibilities. We have to know that these are not the same terms.

But in ministry, we can hardly conceive of a leader who has leadership responsibilities without administrative responsibilities. We can define administration in Christian ministry as *the application of principles derived from Scripture and research to facilitate fulfillment of purpose.*

Three-Dimensional Administration

We can think of administration in different ways. There are three main types of administrative theory. *Conflict analysis*—asking "How does the organization handle conflict?" *Motivation analysis*—"How does the organization motivate people?" And my favorite, *decision-making analysis*—"How are decisions made?" I believe I can tell more about an organization if I find out how decisions are made than in any other way.

Efficiency and Effectiveness

All through our study we want to use the best cutting-edge research as we always stay anchored to our biblical and theological roots. Key administrative processes operate continuously and cyclically. Skills like planning, implementing, and evaluating never end. Our organizational structure and policies must enhance both effectiveness and efficiency.

Peter Drucker began the discussion of what everybody now considers the differences between those two words. *Efficiency is doing things right; effectiveness is doing the right things.* We do not want one or the other—we want both! The words we will use throughout the book are *product* and *process.* Similarly, we could talk about *achievement* and *personality* or *task* and *need.* We deal with the *job* and the *people*; if we don't keep the job and the people in mind all the time, we will run into difficulties along the way.

Leadership can be described as the exercise of one's spiritual gifts to influence a group to identify and achieve ministry-related goals in a given situation. Communicating, stimulating vision, clarifying mission and purpose—all this will come later in our study. First we need to focus on administration. We need to nurture the culture of ministry; build a team-oriented philosophy of ministry; make sure biblical values are honored through the organization or ministry; sustain the heritage rather than just what you have brought to the table; and, one more time, reproduce leadership. There is a difference between leadership and administration, but in ministry we do both all the time.

The Gift of Administration

We deal next with *the gift of administration.* In Scripture, the Greek word (*kybernetes*) is usually translated as "shipmaster, helmsmen." It appears three times in the New Testament: Acts 27:11; 1 Corinthians 12:28; Revelation 18:17. First Corinthians 12 is the only place it describes a spiritual gift. In Romans 12 we read about the gift of leadership. So the gifts of leadership and administration are different, just as the skills of leadership and administration are different.

Four Tasks of Administration

When we look at all the tasks of administrators, we could name six or seven. However, from my study of research, I narrow it down to four. These are not *the* four, but they are four that we commonly see.

First, *involving other people* is of primary importance. This includes *maintaining personnel morale*, a task very strategic in *achieving the goals of the organization* (that's the *product* factor; involving other people and sustaining morale are *process* factors). And finally, *allowing for innovation.* James Kouzes and Barry Posner, who have named five fundamental leadership practices, wisely remind us "Leaders challenge the process."[1] Good leaders do this constantly. Challenging the process doesn't mean being a rebel; it means that you deliberately ask all the time, about everything, "Isn't there a better way to do this?"

In my classes I talk a lot about management and leadership axioms, and I will deal with those from time to time as we go through the course. I listed some of the popular ones below.

Parkinson's Law: *Work expands to fill the time available.* Retired people discover this. We say things like, "I don't know how I ever had time to work, I'm so busy now." That's Parkinson's Law catching us. Work expands to fill the time available.

Miles' Law: *Where you stand depends on where you sit.* That means how you think about things depends on what position you hold in the organization. Sometimes students come to me and say, "My church doesn't work right; it doesn't function anything like what I'm learning in this class. What can I do to fix it?" And the answer is, if you are just someone who sits in the pew, probably nothing but pray. But if you are the pastor or a key ministry leader, maybe I can give you some suggestions. Where you stand depends on where you sit.

Pareto's Law: *The significant elements of a group usually constitute only a small part.* This is the old 80/20 effect that we hear about so often (i.e., 20 percent of the people do 80 percent of the work). A gross generalization, it still helps us grasp the problem of imbalance.

The Law of Effect: *Behaviors immediately rewarded will increase; behaviors immediately punished will decrease.* All parents reading this book should take this home and use it there. The word *immediately* makes the difference.

The Peter Principle: *People tend to be promoted until they reach a level of their incompetence.* Bureaucracies and major corporations keep advancing people until finally they discover they cannot do the job. By the way, this principle is named for its originator, Lawrence Peter; it has nothing to do with Simon Peter.

The Paul Principle: *In a growing organization, positions often grow faster than the people who hold them.* A person might be effective in a job when she takes it, but the organization grows beyond the person. All of a sudden you have someone who has not kept up with the movement of the organization and is no longer effective.

The Pygmalion Principle: *Our expectations for others condition our behavior toward them and affect how they behave toward us.* I will come back to this several times throughout this book. One general idea drawn from this principle is that people usually perform to the level at which they were recruited.

Administration and Leadership Style

TEAM MANAGEMENT

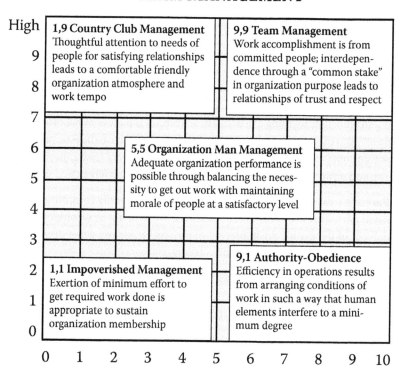

1,9 Country Club Management Thoughtful attention to needs of people for satisfying relationships leads to a comfortable friendly organization atmosphere and work tempo	**9,9 Team Management** Work accomplishment is from committed people; interdependence through a "common stake" in organization purpose leads to relationships of trust and respect
5,5 Organization Man Management Adequate organization performance is possible through balancing the necessity to get out work with maintaining morale of people at a satisfactory level	
1,1 Impoverished Management Exertion of minimum effort to get required work done is appropriate to sustain organization membership	**9,1 Authority-Obedience** Efficiency in operations results from arranging conditions of work in such a way that human elements interfere to a minimum degree

The above model is helpful in understanding administration. The point of this model is to progress in a northeasterly direction toward team management. Moving any other direction (such as straight up the left side or straight across the bottom), or getting stalled in the middle, will bring you grief. You want to go northeast and move all the way on up toward team management.

At 1,1 we experience "impoverished management." Nothing is happening; no goals are achieved. If we roll straight to the right, crushing everyone in the way, we end up with authority/obedience management, which as we saw in chapter 1 is unproductive and unbiblical. Getting stalled in the middle results in "organization man (or woman)" management, basically maintaining the bureaucracy. Rising up the left side may make everyone happy, but it achieves nothing. Remember product and process? Product is the lower right corner and process is the upper left corner. We want neither alone but a happy combination of both—team management.

Administration and Delegation

Delegation does not come naturally to a leader. Moses, a very bright person, very highly schooled in Egypt, never considered using delegation despite his enormous duties. Of course he learned under a very "Old Covenant" leader in the Pharaoh.

Delegation is essential for survival. You can't make it in a major leadership post if you are not willing to give away segments of responsibility.

Delegation is a biblical and spiritual technique. This is particularly obvious in Exodus 18. God sends Jethro to Moses; Moses listens; Moses does it; and things get better.

Delegation does not abrogate the leader's responsibility. Sometimes you have to remind people of this: "I'm not asking other people to do things just so I can get out of work; I have plenty to do." The point is that if you delegate well, you may even have *time to think*: too many leaders do not.

Delegation should be practiced only with competent personnel. Why set someone up for failure? Why deliberately delegate a task you know is too hard for the person to whom you give it? You want to stretch people. But you want to arrange the situation so people are able to achieve what you ask them to achieve.

Delegation requires a span of control. Someone needs to supervise and take care of each person to whom tasks have been delegated. And *delegation results in a harmonious organization*—if people do it right.

Making It Work

In administration, you're always dealing with product (getting the job done); you're always dealing with process (the people who do it with you).

This managerial model helps us understand organizational behavior in educational administration, church administration, school administration, business administration, or any kind of administration. Though based on a conflict model, "conflict" is not used here in a negative sense. The main point

MAN-IN-ORGANIZATION

(A managerial model for understanding organizational behavior
in educational administration, based on a conflict motif.)

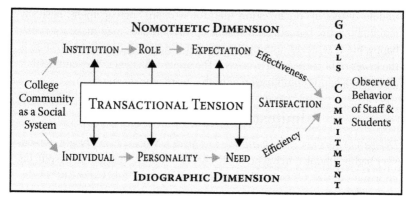

AXIOM: The behavior of an individual (staff or student) within the
social system (college community) results from both the expectations
held by others for him, and from his own personality needs.

is that the elements of product and process are in constant transactional
tension. My work is in colleges and seminaries, so you see that on the
left side I use a college community as a social system. On the top is the
nomothetic dimension, or elements related to product. On the bottom is
the *idiographic* dimension, or elements related to process. For example, the
institution appears on the top and the *individual* below. The *role* expected
of the leader is on top; the *personality* of the leader is on the bottom. *These
elements always remain in tension.*

Maybe you've experienced this but just called it something else. Think
about this course. The course offers *expectations*, but you have *needs*. You
must recognize that these always work together. The hope then is to reach
effectiveness, efficiency, satisfaction, and goal commitment. In this model
the observed behavior of staff and students in a college is the measuring
rod. This diagram originated with Andrew Halpin[2] and it has been one of
my favorite models. I have tinkered with it a bit and come back to it again
and again in my own work.

This model helps us to understand the tension of product and process
in ministry situations. Here is a practical example. Suppose you chair a
missionary committee in a local church, and the role of the committee is to
plan the annual missionary conference. So you work all year to do this. There
are five other members on the committee. A debate arises about which speaker

you should invite, and the issue is not really resolved in the committee. But you need to move ahead, so you take a vote and make the decision.

However, one of the members of the committee feels very unhappy about the way the decision was made and about the speaker that you have invited (the vote was four to one). The conference is terrific. The speaker is great; the international flags come out; the international dinner on Friday night tastes wonderful, and everyone says, "This is the greatest missionary conference we ever had." You smile and think, *Great. Maybe I'll be asked to be chairman again next year.* But then they ask that dissatisfied person on the committee, and she says, "Yes, I agree, this is the greatest missionary conference we have ever had; but I will never again be a member of that committee!" *Process!* Product was the conference. Process is the feelings of the people in the group that planned the product.

The Ten Commandments of Project Management

We conclude with a look at the ten commandments of managing a project. Number one is to *set a goal.* Let's stay with our illustration about the missionary conference. What is our overall goal? An effective missionary conference? Yes, we want to be efficient as we put the conference together, and we want to have an effective missionary conference.

Second, we *determine the project objectives*: speaker effectiveness, attendance at the meetings, several missionary testimonies, increased giving to missions over the next year, and heightened missionary interest. There may be many more, but these give us the idea.

Third, *establish checkpoints, activities, relationships, and time estimates,* basically asking the question, "Who does what, when, and how?"

Fourth, *draw a picture of the project schedule.* This could be a PERT chart or some other kind of planning document. These documents usually include the specific activities (or tasks) in the project, sequence of activities, time required for each activity, milestones marking completion, and total project time. In all good leadership books you can find different kinds of planning documents for how you get from the beginning of a project to the conclusion.

Fifth, *direct people individually and as a project team.* "Leaders encourage the heart" (another leadership practice from Kouzes and Posner).[3] Leaders challenge the process, but leaders also encourage the heart. This involves the sixth step, which is to *reinforce the commitment and excitement of the project team.* This is a key leadership role.

The seventh and eighth steps go together. *Keep everyone who is connected with the project informed* and *build agreements that vitalize team members*; you need consensus on vital issues at all times. Here again is process—

working with people, making them happy that they belong to the team. This is not just crucial; it is ongoing. Some of us are oriented toward product and some toward process. The point is that we have to learn to do the one that comes with greater difficulty. I confess I am a product person. I have to force myself to spend time with people, show concern for people, watch out for people. My son is process-oriented, and he is a Vice President of Spiritual Formation in a college. He has to be sure he doesn't just stand around talking to people all the time because, as a high-level administrator, he has to pay attention to product. Transactional balance must always be there.

Ninth, *empower yourself and others on the project team.* I will talk about that more later. The only way to empower people is to give them some of your power. Be thinking about that. This will naturally lead to the tenth step, which is to *encourage risk taking and creativity.* One way of encouraging risk taking is to give rewards for *good* mistakes, "You did it wrong; it didn't work. Never mind, it was a great idea. We'll tweak it; we'll make some changes. We'll be able to do it better next time." You never say, "Oh no, you failed. Do it the way we've always done it. Don't make any changes. It worked last year; it will work this year." You reward people for creative ideas.

Wrap-Up

No matter what ministry leadership role you fulfill, you will probably have responsibilities of both leadership and administration. Leadership and administration are different, but they are both spiritual gifts. Any good administrator must pay attention to both the *process* and the *product.* If we don't keep both the job and the people in mind all the time, we will run into difficulties along the way in our leadership style, delegation, and project management.

Digging Deeper

1. Describe the difference between efficiency and effectiveness. Why are both important?

2. Why do you think Paul chose "shipmaster" as the word to describe administration?

3. What does it mean for a leader to "challenge the process"? Why is this sometimes difficult?

4. How would you differentiate between the terms *administration* and *leadership*?

5. Describe the difference between "process" and "product." Why must these factors receive equal attention?

Notes

[1] James M. Kouzes and Barry Z. Posner, *The Leadership Challenge* (San Francisco: Jossey-Bass, 1995), 18.

[2] Andrew W. Halpin, *Theory and Research in Administration* (New York: Macmillan, 1966), 83.

[3] Kouzes and Posner, *Leadership Challenge*, 18.

ORGANIZING YOUR
MEANINGFUL MINISTRY

"You and these people who come to you will only wear yourselves out.
The work is too heavy for you; you cannot handle it alone." (Ex. 18:18)

3

Moses' father-in-law, Jethro, may have been the first management consultant in history. Moses was burning out and his people with him when Jethro dropped by to offer some help on reorganizing the troops. Organizing provides the foundational function of administrative leadership. The disorganized person cannot really be effective and efficient in most areas. How can a disorganized person do long-range planning? So we put organizing close to the front of the book. Every pastoral survey I have seen shows frustration with administrative duties. Pastors surely know they have to do administration, but most have not trained for it, so when they face it they find difficulties. I assume this is also the case with other ministry leaders in the church.

Think back with me to the three ways of looking at leadership from chapter 1. These relate to how you organize yourself and your work. Leadership involves the possession of *certain personality traits and abilities*. But leadership does not rest solely on the idea of the so-called strong natural leader. Leadership also means *meeting group needs and fulfilling group goals*. Leadership is always related to the group you serve, and that takes us back to the product/process dialogue again. Finally, leadership is the *ability to solve problems in a given situation*. Leadership is always situational; you already know that. Problem-solving and decision-making are central in all kinds of leadership.

The Three Common Qualities
of Effective Organizations

The diagram below is typical of the way I teach. I use a number of these overlapping circles or ovals. Effective organizations have three qualities in common regarding their values. *Clarity* means what people believe in, *a clear mission*. Some churches are committed to world evangelization; that's what they do and what they believe in.

Consensus: how well people agree about what they believe in. Just think how many people go to church on Sunday morning and readily say, "I believe in the Bible," but don't really know what the Bible says. They have never read the Bible from cover to cover. You probably know dozens of folks like that. Effective organizations are made up of people who know with clarity what the mission is and are agreed about the mission.

Conviction: strong feelings about doctrine and behavior. This presents another way of discussing theology of church ministry. Good church ministries have core values; they agree on their core values; and they have complete conviction in their core values.

One of my core values (and you may not agree with this) is the importance of hymnody in Christianity. Hymnody has all but disappeared from today's churches. I take the view that for several hundred years Christians have learned their theology as much from hymns as from preaching. When we take away the hymns and use only worship choruses (some of which are very good and some of which are very bad), we also take away much of the theology. Of course, let me also say that some hymns are very good and some just plain insipid. But in general, the theology of hymns is much greater than the theology of worship choruses. I don't want to debate that issue here, but it's a good example of a core value. As you organize your ministry, you will need to think about the core values and determine how to promote clarity, consensus, and conviction among those involved.

Effective organizations have three qualities in common regarding their values . . .

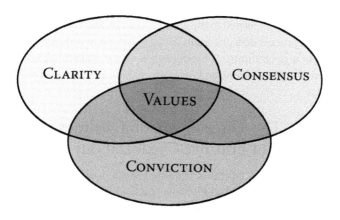

Organization and Ministry Control

A key factor in organization is attaining ministry control. In secular settings, this might be called job control. You have ministry control if you have *adequate* resources. Not control over people but control of your ministry, the ability to do it and do it well. Take the yoke; share the burden. This is the taking-the-yoke part.

First, you need a *grasp of goals.* "What are we charged with doing?" Perhaps you have served on committees and heard the chairperson say, "We're not really sure what we're supposed to do. Does anybody on this committee understand our task? Let's call the pastor and find out." You can't have ministry control if you don't have a grasp of your goals.

You can't have ministry control unless you have adequate *human resources* (personnel) to do it. Maybe this will take just one part-time assistant or perhaps a whole parcel of volunteers or staff. My job as Dean of the Faculty and Vice President at Dallas Seminary required five full-time people in my office. We were supervising every aspect of academic operations for a seminary (at that time) of sixteen hundred students, and we needed every one of those people.

Financial resources. This does not always mean millions of dollars; it doesn't mean the children's ministry you are leading needs an unlimited budget. You just need *adequate* financial resources to do what God has called you to do. God provides what you have, and He expects you to be a good steward of that. Good stewardship of your financial resources helps make ministry control possible.

Equipment. Here again, why think so big? You don't need every electronic gadget; you just need whatever is necessary to do the job. The word *necessary* is key. God's servants must have the equipment that they need, and as a leader, you need to make that possible.

Time is enormously important, and that's what this chapter is really about. If you do not have adequate time, you cannot gain ministry control, and you may go home every night, every week, every month, and every year saying, "I just don't have time. I'm so tired. I'm exhausted. I don't have time." Part of that might be because you're taking the yoke but not sharing the burden, and part of it may be because you're not using your time well.

Finally, *confidence.* Confidence doesn't come unless you have achieved the things above it in this list. *And ministry control rarely comes in less than a year.* That's why constant ministry moves are a curse. Some denominations change pastors every three years. That's their statistical average. The average tenure of associate staff is eighteen months, nationwide. Youth directors, children's ministry directors, music ministry directors—eighteen months!

They barely find all the rooms in that time. You cannot do ministry that way.

When you agree to a ministry, stay there. Ministry control will not likely come in less than a year because there are events in the ministry calendar that you don't know about until you experience them in their unique time slots. In a youth ministry, it could be a fall football game outreach, a winter retreat, a summer mission trip. Not less than a year, and sometimes longer. Ask God to let you gain experience and build confidence. To do that you need good foundations, reasonable expectations, an accurate job description, and the ability to delegate.

Analyzing Your Activities

This activity analysis is enormously useful and foundational to leadership decision-making. It provides the drivers' manual for organization and we read it across, line by line.

ACTIVITY ANALYSIS			
A	**B**	**C**	**D**
Intrinsic Importance			
1. Very Important Absolutely MUST be done	Important Should be done	Of Small Importance May be useful	Unimportant Can be eliminated
Urgency			
2. Very Urgent Must be done NOW	Urgent Should be done soon	Not Urgent May be done later	Time Not a Factor May be done anytime
Delegation			
3. Must be Done by Me I am only person who can do it	Can be Delegated to A	Can be Delegated to B **Volunteer or Assistant**	Can be Delegated to C
Personal Contacts			
4. People I Must See Each Day	People I Must See Weekly	People to See Regularly	People to See Infrequently

First we watch for areas of *intrinsic importance*. There are 1A items that must be done and 1D items that can be eliminated. I can tell you that people are better at spotting 1A items than they are 1D items. If you know anything at all about your ministry, you know those things that are very important and absolutely must be done. But you will find it harder to spot those nagging little things at the corner of the desk or in the bottom drawer, and then to admit they are unimportant and can be eliminated. But effective activity analysis requires just that.

Careful, just because something is 1A does not mean it is also 2A. It could be "very important," but it might not necessarily need to be "done now." So, now we have a two-way item: A, it must be done *now*, or it's urgent; it should be done *soon* under B; it's not urgent and it may be done *later* under C; or D, time is not a factor—it may be done *anytime*. You know what will happen to a 2D item; it will likely never get done. So perhaps 1A items can become 2D items, but it is not necessary that 1A items are also 2A. You might consider something very important, but you might be able to do it next week, next month, or maybe even next year.

Line three is different from lines one and two in that it designates four different levels. Three really just asks one question: "Must this be done by me?" And if you say yes, you do it; if you say no, then the next question is "To whom can it be delegated? To A, B, or C?" These important people may include an administrative assistant, another leader, a ministry volunteer, even a spouse or child. Just because you don't have a staff does not mean you can't delegate. The heart of church ministry is volunteerism, and leading and developing volunteers is the main focus in this course.

And finally, analyze your *personal contacts.* People you have to see every day, a 4A item; people you must see weekly; people to see regularly; people to see infrequently—you have to decide who fits in which category.

Choosing a Leadership Style That Fits

An important part of organizing your ministry is intentionally deciding upon your leadership style (as explained in chapter 1). Will you lead with an autocratic style, a free rein style, or a team leadership style? When you select your leadership style, you take certain things into consideration. You can't choose a leadership style unless you know your organization and its climate.

♦ FOLLOWERS: Knowing the makeup of the group you will be leading is important. What is the average age of the group? Are they newcomers to the ministry or have they been serving for a while? What percentage of the group is male or female? What is the history and cultural orientation of the group?

- ♦ TASK: What is the nature of the task you are leading them into? Does it require training? Can people accept and apply empowerment? Do they understand what you expect of them?

- ♦ ORGANIZATION: What is the personality of the organization in which you are called to lead? What is its history? How would you describe the organizational style and polity? Can the organization understand a team approach, or would you seem like a person from Mars if you came in to model and teach servant leadership?

- ♦ ENVIRONMENT: Consider both internal and external factors. Is the environment friendly or hostile? Is it cooperative or competitive?

- ♦ OTHER LEADERS: What is the prominent leadership style of the other leaders with whom you will serve? What is the decision-making process? Is there team potential? How long will it take to develop leadership teams?

Organizing Your Time

Let me take you quickly through eleven tips of effectiveness. Don't try to do these all at once; work them into your life piece by piece.

1. Understand how objectives and goals operate.

We start here. The key is *increasing specificity.* You get more specific as you approach the event, and remember, without priorities, goals are feeble. The next chapter discusses goal setting extensively.

2. Clarify your lifetime objectives.

This can only be done after some experience and maturity. Age is a component, but you also need some ministry background. I would suggest ten years of ministry background before you can really deal with this, but you can start thinking about it now if you're not yet there. I tackled this analysis when I was thirty-five and found it very effective. You ask some basic questions: "What does God want from me? How has God gifted me?" and "Where is God calling me?"

There are two other questions that form yet another axiom of leadership. Actually it's only one question because you might not need question two. If you're thinking about leaving a ministry post, you must know, "Is God finished with me here?" Never mind my problems; never mind the people who give me trouble; "Is God finished with me here?" If the answer is no, then you need not ask the other question. If the answer is yes, then you ask, "Where does He want me next?"

3. Analyze how you spend your time now.

To do this, use the time and activity analysis grid we looked at earlier. I suggest that you inventory your life for at least one week in thirty-minute increments. Try to select a normal week (if you have normal weeks). For me February was always the most normal of months; I did the fewest unusual things in February. Remember priorities. You waste time when you do not use most of your time to achieve your key goals. That's why so many people don't like committees, because committees often get trapped in this particular problem.

4. Inventory what future work you know about, estimate time, and set priorities.

I try to do this on a daily basis. I write down at the end of every day things I need to do the next day, prioritize those items, and then go after them. Of course there are interruptions, and we will deal with those next.

5. Eliminate time wasters that clutter your life.

Some common time wasters are meetings, procrastination, daydreaming, the telephone, crises, inability to say no, interruptions, fire-fighting, and indecision. You need your own list. But here's another axiom for you: *group like tasks.* Do common things together. Make your telephone calls at the same time. Often people will make a telephone call, write a letter, meet with a visitor, and then do something else. But every time you switch tasks you lose mental concentration and time. Designate a time to make telephone calls. Write your letters at a certain time. Group like tasks and fight these time-wasters that clutter up your time.

Do not let the telephone control your life. Since everyone has a cell phone now, people can reach you and say, "Oh, hi, I'm riding on a bus and I've got an hour with nothing to do, so I thought I'd talk to you." Well, you are not on a bus; you have something very important on your desk. Just because that person owns a phone does not mean he or she has priority in your life.

6. Analyze your activities.

Again, refer to the grid we looked at earlier: what is most important, what is most urgent, and so on. Goals are useless without priorities. Failure to have priorities creates frustration. Suppose you have five goals; you write them down, and you achieve four during a certain day. But if the one you did *not* achieve was the most important, it has not been a good day.

7. Delegate whenever and wherever possible.

Failure to delegate is not a rational problem. People do not decide, "I really want to do all the work myself so that I can be frustrated and stressed. Then I can go to my doctor and tell him how stressed out I am, get on some medication, and eventually die young. That's my plan." You are not that irrational. Failure to delegate is an emotional problem. People make judgments about work; they take the yoke, but they don't share the burden and end up frustrated. *Empowerment is the best step toward building new leadership, and delegation usually results in empowerment.*

8. Practice self-discipline in the use of time.

Do this in the way you talk, in your eating behavior, and in completing your responsibilities. "America is an obese nation," we are told over and over again on the news—a nation of people twenty, thirty, forty pounds overweight. Often this simply reflects lack of discipline. Certainly there could be a medical problem that causes it, but lack of discipline creates terrible problems for leaders. Friend, you are leading in an undisciplined world, and only disciplined people can do that. Read 1 and 2 Timothy; the same quality was needed in the first century.

9. Centralize your calendar and appointment information.

For some of you this might not mean much now, but when you accept a major leadership position, the people closest to you (such as your spouse, your children, or other family members) need to know where you are at all times. If you have an administrative assistant, or secretary, this person should also know. I think an assistant is indispensable, even a part-time volunteer who works ten hours a week. I admit to being a staff-driven leader. You can imagine with five full-time people in my office, they told me what to do and where to go. One assistant might say, "You have a meeting at 2:00; here's the folder; this is what you need to do; here's the agenda; here are the issues; this is what we agreed you would emphasize," and I'm off. I had seven meetings a week and chaired four of them, so you can imagine the stress level if I tried to control all that on my own. We call this calendar coordination, and it requires consistent note-keeping. It matters not if you use a piece of scrap paper, a Palm Pilot, or a Blackberry—whatever works.

10. Concentrate on productivity, not activity.

That's an axiom. Concentrate on productivity (getting things done), not activity (being busy). Design work schedules and patterns that work for you. You may not always have that choice; sometimes people tell you what to do and when to do it. But when you have the choice, leadership begins to show up—*discretional use of time demands maturity.*

Concentrate on productivity, not activity. Group like tasks and decide where your preferences are. Are you a night person or a morning person? As a night person, I have been persecuted by morning people all my life. You know the type—people who get up at 5:00 a.m. and run ten miles, then read the Bible for two hours and wonder how I can call myself a Christian if I don't do that. The simple truth? I cannot function in the morning.

But at night I am in good shape. Anytime from 7:00 until midnight my juices are flowing and I can do all kinds of work. Years ago I finally admitted that. I became comfortable with it and decided to take no more abuse from morning people. They're an abusive bunch (I apologize to all you morning people).

Do you work best at home or at your office? I have written fifty-three books (edited or co-edited; authored or co-authored), and I never wrote a book or any part of a book at the office. That was always done at home. I had to make time at home in my study to do it because I dedicated my office to administration and preparation for teaching. Home was the place for writing. Obviously I tried to spend as much time at home as possible, and the only way that could be done was by being efficient and effective at the office and having a great staff.

And then the matter of handling information, on a computer or in books and magazines—filing, researching, word processing. Where you file information is crucial. Filing is not the question here; anyone can file. Retrieval makes the difference. If you can't find what you need when you need it, filing is nothing more than storage.

11. Make all research do double and triple duty.

I am amazed how much time and material people waste. Again, this requires an effective filing and retrieval system, but don't waste the fruit of your study time. I assume that when I spend four, five, twenty hours in Bible study, the results of that will show up in sermons, in Bible studies, in writing, and on my radio broadcast. I'm going to make at least *quadruple use* of that study.

Wrap-Up

This chapter offers a great deal to digest and practice. As I have already said, don't frustrate yourself by trying to do it all at once. Recognize that the activities of chapter 3 depend upon the attitudes of chapter 1. *Leadership is learned behavior,* and some of us take longer to learn it than others. Pick three or four items in the chapter and begin to work on them. And remember, we still have nine chapters to come! Maybe some of the following questions will give you an idea or two.

Digging Deeper

1. Do you believe you have the gift of administration? How do you know?

2. Do you think you have ministry control? If not, what's missing?

3. Take a shot at analyzing your activities. Can you determine priorities from using this chart?

4. What leadership style would work best in your current ministry situation? How might you move people toward team leadership?

5. What are the biggest problems you face in managing your time? How can they be minimized or eliminated?

Setting and Achieving Goals

"I press toward the goal for the prize of the upward call of God in Christ Jesus." (Phil. 3:14, ESV)

4

Every organization has goals. You may wonder if your ministry really has any idea where it is headed or why. But you should assume that an organization has goals even if they have not been written, rethought, or brought up to date in ten or twenty years. People have some idea where they want to go.

You should also assume that the organization has some form of structure to facilitate goal realization. That might be an overt structure with charts and graphics familiar to everyone, or it might be something discarded or put in the bottom drawer somewhere.

Finally, you should assume that the organization requires effective administration if goals are to be reached. If you have read the first three chapters carefully, you know that connection. Goal achievement is impossible without appropriate administration.

Doing Things on Purpose

Purpose provides an organization with a will to live now. That does not mean a will to *live* now rather than to *die* now; it means a will to live *now* rather than only in the past or in the future. Some churches live in the past, but others only live in the future. They like to say, "We don't have anything now, but in ten years this will be a great church." Forward thinking certainly beats nostalgia, but there is a here-and-now ministry; Jesus could come at any time, and we must decide what we should do right now.

Purpose provides enthusiasm if our goals are achievable. If they are not, we face trouble, because *few things are more demoralizing in an organization than a history of unachieved goals.*

Effectiveness and efficiency come because of prioritization. Objectives give us the only basis for evaluation—if the goals are measurable. They also force planning, because objectives and planning are Siamese twins. A goal needs a plan to make it work. We can only achieve ministry targets when goals are "claimed"; someone must step up and take responsibility.

Purpose gives us an emphasis on productivity rather than activity. Purpose also provides a measure of progress. As we achieve a goal we move on to the next goal, then to the next, and progress results. Struggling groups will see a reduction in conflict when everyone moves toward the same goals.

Enhancing Your Purpose and Vision

Every leader should determine his or her lifetime purposes. It is helpful to write these down on paper and identify six or seven key areas, such as family, ministry, spiritual growth, career, and so on. *Purpose* is just a synonym for *mission.* Each of your lifetime purposes should yield specific objectives, from which you can develop goals and action steps. Once you have this document, you can periodically look at it during your life to see to what extent each goal has been achieved.

You should also think about your present ministry, whatever you do, wherever you do it, and whatever title you hold. Determine what God wants from you here and now. Write a paragraph on how God has used you so far. You should ascertain your spiritual gifts, ministry experiences, and what God has done for you through the years. Then write a paragraph describing your future *vision* (not for your ministry, but for yourself), a paragraph describing where you serve and what more you can do there.

Test your assumptions with others, obviously with a spouse, but also with your supervisor, with the elders, with ministry co-leaders or volunteers, or with friends, and see what kind of feedback you get. Use mental rehearsal. Mental rehearsal has to do with what we used to call "psycho-cybernetics," the idea of trying to mentally project yourself into the next day or into the next event to anticipate what potential issues or problems might come up. Unfortunately, I learned psycho-cybernetics to a fault, and acquired insomnia in the process. So I lie awake at night using mental rehearsal about meetings and issues coming up the next day. I don't recommend it to that degree. After you are sure of your goals, pray specifically about them.

Mission—The Heart of Ministry

Please do not confuse *mission* and *vision. Mission* defines why your church or ministry program exists. *Vision* describes what you will do about it in the future. So mission stands at the beginning of the process and vision at the end. Mission is asking, "Why do we exist? What is our basic purpose? How is our ministry unique or distinctive? Who are our principle 'stakeholders'?" The word *stakeholders* is used today to describe people who have significant interest in an organization: the publics, the customers, the clients, the users.

What are our principle services/products, present and future? What does our ministry offer? What does it offer now, and what do we expect it to offer in the future? There may have been a time when your church had no intention of starting a daughter church. Somewhere along the line that became a future goal as a part of the congregation's mission.

What are our principle market segments? Whom do we serve now and in the future? What are our principle outlets and distribution channels, present and future?

Where and how can we do what we think God has called us to do? John Wesley used to say, "The world is my parish." But that was not true. He saw very little of the world. He may have prayed for the whole world, but small portions of North America and England formed his parish. Almost every organization is geographically bound.

What is different about our ministry from what it was between three and five years ago? What have we changed, and what will likely be different three to five years in the future? You can see already why goal-setting and planning are inseparably linked.

Ministry By Objectives

MBO. I call this Ministry By Objectives, a take-off from Management By Objectives. This process of managing rests upon identifying purposes, objectives, and desired results; establishing a program for obtaining those results; and evaluating the outcomes. I've offered ten steps toward employing Ministry By Objectives in a specific ministry setting.

1. Define your purpose and mission.

2. Realistically assess your ministry's strengths and weaknesses.

3. Write specific and measurable objectives for your key ministry areas.

4. Work to obtain a general agreement on your objectives.

5. Strive to attain ministry control as quickly as possible. (See chapter 3.)

6. Develop strategies on how best to use available resources to meet your objectives.

7. Require accountability all through the organization.

8. Design long- and short-range plans.

9. Be willing to change or modify objectives, plans, or strategies as situation variables may require.

10. Measure progress all along the way.

As you think about objectives, always keep this in mind: There is a single purpose (or mission), but there are always multiple objectives; there are always multiple goals stemming from each objective, and multiple action steps arising from each goal.

Remember that your objectives must be derived from what your ministry is, what it will be, and what it should be. Objectives must be capable of conversion into specific targets and assignments. They must make possible concentration of resources and efforts. We have limited people, limited finances, and limited space. We cannot afford to make blind decisions regarding where these precious resources go. We concentrate them on the basis of prioritized objectives. *Objectives must relate to all areas on which the survival of your ministry depends.* Don't forget that every area of your ministry must have its own objectives. Leave out any part, and you will corrupt the effectiveness of the rest of the organization.

Are You Problem-Oriented or Objective-Oriented?

You can ask questions to determine your orientation and then select ways to develop new orientation. For example, what percentage of your business or planning sessions focuses on problems? Are you a problem-centered ministry? If you think that is possible, try following a few simple guidelines:

1. Organize the decision-making process to aim at objectives.

2. Eliminate timidity. Get people to say what they think.

3. Structure group decision-making.

4. Eliminate long lead times between the setting of objectives and targeted completion dates. You really can't set ministry objectives for a year ahead and then not look at them for a year. You set the targets, and then you revisit them at least monthly to check your progress.

Control Your Priorities

Effective ministries identify and act on their real priorities. They turn their priorities into goals, and then prioritize those goals. Goal-oriented leaders control the obstacles that sidetrack ministry. Don't let them rule you. We've already talked about that in chapter 3. Communicate effectively with those who work with you. Every organization needs ministry teams talking to each other. We teach them to relate to each other, not to try to guard their own turf while being seemingly unconcerned about the rest of the ministry. Delegate and negotiate tasks that can be done effectively by someone else. *Delegation is not doing all you can and giving away the rest; it is giving away everything you can and doing the rest.*

Never Forget the Informal Organization

The questions you ask to spot the informal organization (anything you don't find on the organizational chart) include how people are recruited in the organization, how decisions are made, how goals are shared, how problems are solved, and how information is disseminated.

Few documents in most organizations tell how information is disseminated, but we all know it happens through the administrative, or secretarial, staff. No group knows more about the organization when they pool their information than the administrative assistants of the various leaders. That's a powerful pack; they know what's going on. Any one of them may only know details in his or her area; but when they get together, they can draw the big picture.

Take Care of Your Administrative Assistant

If you are in a leadership position that includes a personal assistant, you have a valuable tool to aid you in achieving goals. I have already told you I am a staff-driven leader. I take my assistant into my confidence on almost every issue. I'm interested in her opinion. I want her to know what I'm thinking, why I'm thinking that way, and find out whether she agrees. I want her feedback and participation in the goals of the ministry. I would never have a staff meeting without my assistant there. I place great importance on all staff members. I hire them. I train them. I hold high expectations for them. And I expect them to hold me to a high standard.

I asked one of my past assistants, Debbie Puckett, to talk to me about her job. I had never been an assistant, so it would be foolish for me to try to describe it myself. Debbie had been with me several years when I asked her, "What does an assistant want from his or her boss?" Below is a summary of what she said:

Opportunities to work independently. In other words, "Don't look over my shoulder all the time. Tell me what to do; then let me do it."

Clear expectations. I tried to identify not only what the tasks were for a given week or day but to establish priorities as well. I don't want that responsibility on my assistant's shoulders. Not that she couldn't get it right; I just don't want her to waste time thinking about that. I'll set the priorities and number items accordingly.

A regular meeting time. I would never lead an organization without requiring weekly staff meetings. They don't have to last much longer than an hour, sometimes not even that long. I always have food there, and we always have a time of spiritual thinking, praying for one another, discussing the tasks we are doing, asking how we can help each other, and really developing a team spirit.

Rush jobs in emergency only. Assistants do not like to work for leaders who practice crisis management, leaders who are always putting out fires, leaders for whom everything must be done right now. If this describes you, you may be a micromanager so busy with little details you fail to see the big picture and plan ahead. I have discovered that if I keep assistants well ahead of the game all the time, when I do have an emergency rush job, they are quite willing to stay or take it home and get it done on time.

Proper equipment is very important. As I mentioned in the last chapter, equipment is part of ministry control. Your responsibility as a leader is to see that the people under your care have the necessary equipment to do their jobs well.

Encouragement and appreciation are crucial. Encouraging the hearts of other people is probably the most important thing that a leader does. And it is not only cheap, it's free.

Periodic honest evaluation should be done on at least an annual basis. If one of your team members has a problem or is struggling somewhere along the way, then perhaps it's important to deal with it more frequently than just annually.

Good communication regarding the boss's schedule. If you have an assistant, even a ten-hour volunteer, that person needs to know where you are when you are away from the office. Tell that person *where* you are going, *when* you will be back, and *why*.

I thought the last one was interesting. *Interest in the assistant as a person.* That is, relating to this person as someone other than just an employee. You want people to know you see them as people. You ask questions about their children. You're concerned about their health. If they seem to be ill or excessively tired, you inquire if maybe they ought to go home early or take a day off.

Protect Your People

Good leaders build a team of people around them who are committed to the ministry and can help them envision and accomplish ministry goals. Once this team is set up, a leader must work to protect the team members. Leaders protect those people who cannot protect themselves, and they especially guard their staff and ministry volunteers from their own (the leaders') supervisors.

On one occasion my boss told me to fire one of the people who served under me—and to do it by the end of the week. I said no. I was told, "Of course you know it's a simple thing for us to fire you and then we'll fire him."

I responded, "I know that exactly, and that's just what you are going to have to do if you want him gone by Friday. Let's go that route and you won't hear any complaining from me. But the way I see this particular situation, I will not release this person." We did release him three months later, after I had assisted him in finding another position.

It may look as though I was being insubordinate. But telling a person on Wednesday that he's finished on Friday is not Christian leadership behavior, and I won't do it. If it costs me my job to stand up for that principle, so be it. Fire me then fire him and we can go job hunting together! As I said, we found him an acceptable position. That was perhaps twenty years ago, and he is still in the same city. We still stay in contact, and you can bet he remembers the day his boss stood up for him, laying his own job on the line in the process.

Good leaders protect their people more than they protect their buildings, their desks, their papers, their files, their computers, and all other nonhuman resources. *No resource in a ministry organization is more important for the fulfillment of objectives than people.* If you don't have good people, then it really doesn't matter what else you have. A good computer is not going to solve your problems. Good people may.

But we should not end on a negative note. Objectives are very important. They flow from the mission, become goals, and lead into action steps: a singular mission, multiple objectives, multiple goals, multiple actions steps. The key? *Increasing specificity.* In the action step phase we can actually say yes or no; we did it or we didn't do it. The mission is general. Action steps are highly specific.

Wrap-Up

This chapter contains one central goal: that you understand the role of a mission statement, and the use of objectives, goals, and action steps in the leadership process. As you apply this material to your situation, remember to start small. Avoid the thought that you must change the church or ministry program in a week, or a year. Begin slowly and carefully to build around you a cadre of people who can help you think about where your collective ministry should be in the future.

Digging Deeper

1. How would you explain the difference between objectives and goals?

2. State a sample mission statement. Discuss or list at least four objectives for accomplishing the mission. Then list a few goals for each objective and a few action steps for each goal.

3. From observations in meetings and informal discussions, do you consider your ministry organization objective-oriented or problem-oriented? If the latter seems true, what can you do to change it?

4. We have spoken often of "being in control of your priorities." What does that mean, and how do you intend to do it?

5. Why are people important to the fulfillment of objectives? In what ways can you care for and protect the people in your ministry?

PERCEIVING AND
PLANNING MINISTRY

"Plans are established by counsel . . . ." (Prov. 20:18, ESV)

5

A goal needs a plan to make it work. Just think about Joseph in Egypt. "Pharaoh," said he, "we have a problem. We will have seven years of bountiful crops, followed by seven years of famine. That's a fact. The goal is to try to stay alive during the second seven years."

Pharaoh said, "What's the plan? I need a man with a plan, and Joseph, you are my man!"

Planning Principles

Planning is *predetermining a course of action*. But note several principles here. *Planning is an investment, not an expenditure of time*, like reading a map before you start a trip. You need to know what highways you will take, whether you ought to go north or south, if there is a bypass around large towns, or if the interstate is clogged at a certain place. Many people (including leaders) simply don't practice this. They try something, try something else, try something different, and finally use whatever works. That trial-and-error approach leads to a great deal of wasted time.

Consider a second principle—*planning is cyclically based on evaluation*. The better your data, the better your plan. If you have poor evaluation information, you are likely to have a poor plan. Keep good records, and keep them where they can be found. Remember, research always precedes planning.

Planning should allow for maximal participation because participation increases cooperation and decreases resistance. The more people there are who get involved in the planning process, the more likely you can build team consensus. That does not mean the whole church, the whole ministry team, or the whole mission board becomes one big planning committee. It means people know the members of the planning committee, have access to them, and can voice their opinions when they wish.

Planning requires acting intentionally toward goal realization. Picture a student selecting college courses. He should not do so randomly. I have known students who select courses because of what hour or day they fall; but if they intend to earn a degree, they must take the courses the catalog requires. Students should aim toward a specific goal. I get frustrated on some boards or committees. They go through a meeting and talk about something good they want to do, but they do not fix a date and responsibility. They fail to say when it must be done, and they fail to say who is supposed to do it. In those meetings I often say, "Mr. Chairman, could you give us an idea which one of us is responsible for doing this and when it should be done?" Sometimes I get good answers and sometimes I do not. When I chair a meeting I ask that such information be put right in the minutes.

Planning increases in specificity as the event draws nearer. Think about a one year plan; we could go back to that missionary conference we talked about earlier as an example. During the early days of planning, right after this year's missionary conference, we just talk in generalities—meeting together, getting to know the members of the committee, suggesting objectives and outcomes to accomplish. Be careful of two points here: One, do not stay general too long or you cannot get the job done. And two, do not get specific too soon or you may decide too many things that could change before the actual event occurs. *Planning is not an event, it's a process.* The product is your final destination, the goal realization. The process is the path you take in your planning over the course of the year.

Planning requires careful attention to immediate choices. That is because immediate choices determine future options. Suppose you are that student we talked about earlier. You have a Pastoral Ministries major, and you know you must take Greek. Greek is offered as Greek I and Greek II. If you plan to take Greek II, you need a plan to complete Greek I before your senior year, or you will have no time left to take Greek II. A simple illustration, but it shows us we must make immediate choices in light of the mission and the vision, in light of the beginning and the end, because our immediate choices determine future options. How obviously this principle applies to marriage. In college you could look at three people and think any one of them might make a good wife or husband. But when you say "I do," if you are a serious Bible-believing Christian, your immediate choices have greatly narrowed your future options!

Common Pitfalls in Planning

One of the pitfalls is *failure to make the tough decisions.* Good planners are good decision-makers, and people who cannot make decisions, especially tough decisions like budget cuts, do not plan well. *Sloppy data collection and analysis* is another pitfall in planning. If you have bad information from the last five years, you cannot do good planning for next year. *Bureaucratic centralization,* another pitfall, means all the planning is played "close to the vest," as they say, by the bigwigs "in those smoke-filled rooms up on the top floor in the executive suite." The best planning is done by those closest to the fire, not those who know only second- or third-hand what the issues are.

Failure to keep involved parties informed poses a very common problem in planning. We need reports from the planning committee, repeated reports—maybe not every week, but on a regular basis. And then *timidity,* or *lack of vision,* also inhibits good planning. You cannot afford having people on the planning committee whose first response to a new idea is "No, we can't do that; we haven't got enough money; we haven't got enough people; we haven't got enough space." The planning committee should be made up of people who can take a broad view. Yes, you may have to cut back later, but in the early stages of planning consider only the great possibilities of the future.

Beginning with the Basics

These are things you know. *Planning begins with dynamic extrapolation of trends from past and present data.* Look at the demographics. Look at internal and external factors. You need to know where the culture is headed. Students often ask me what magazines and journals I read. Well, I read a lot of magazines and journals, but if you forced me to cut it down to two magazines, they would be *Newsweek* and *Christianity Today.* Why? Because *Newsweek* tells me what is happening in the world, and *Christianity Today* tells me what is happening in the church. You have to know both to stay on the cutting edge of planning.

You need a clear mission statement, a mission statement that passes what we call "the T-shirt test." You should be able to write your mission on a T-shirt. The mission should be so clear that you can state it in one short paragraph; put it on a 3x5 card and tack it to the wall; place it in the bulletin every Sunday.

What about a *diversity of ministry viewpoints*? This stimulates the planning process because the planning committee should be a group in which every member can think ahead. You need a diversity of viewpoints or it won't work. If, for instance, everyone on a planning committee for a church women's retreat is middle-aged, married, and a mother of teenage children, the committee may fail to address the ministry needs of young, single women or women with small children. If everyone on a music planning committee loves choruses but rolls their eyes that some church members prefer hymns, it's time to get a couple of new members to represent other viewpoints in the congregation.

Planning models abound, and you see one of them here: "Steps in Planning." No need to describe this in detail, except to ask you to pay careful attention to the arrows. The diagram assumes a steady flow from information gathering to the plan.

Steps in Planning

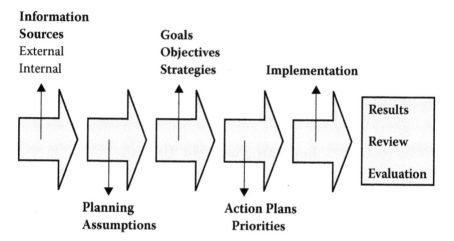

Information Sources
External
Internal

Goals
Objectives
Strategies

Implementation

Results

Review

Evaluation

Planning Assumptions

Action Plans Priorities

Information sources are both *internal* and *external*. Internal means within your church or specific ministry. External refers to your neighborhood, your town, your state, your general environment. Thirty years ago much of this was pure guesswork. We talked about external demographics and said, "Well, maybe this will happen and maybe not." Now you can read *National Demographics*, and every city planning commission has demographic information you can get your hands on.

From them you develop your *planning assumptions*. Then the *goals*, *objectives* and *strategies*, *action plans*, and *priorities* come before implementation. Do not be confused by the jargon and the managerial terms. Picture how this happens because the *results*, the *review* and the *evaluation* (out in that little rectangular box), mean that we can now go back and do it all again. We review our assumptions to see if they were correct, review our goals and objectives, and measure whether we thought and did the right things.

The simplest planning effort is for one year. Even though you have only one mission, there are probably five or six areas in which any church or ministry has to plan for the next year. Objectives must cover every area of your ministry. You can't leave anything out.

Reasons to Plan

Why plan? Because *planning makes possible a good beginning.* Planning gets us started in the year. Annual planning is the easiest and most logical place to start. I have been part of a planning team that looked as far as fifteen years ahead. That was next to impossible and took years to achieve. By the time we got it together it was a ten-year plan, and even that was very ambitious. If you have never done serious planning before, stick with one year. After you get comfortable with the process, you might get by with three to five years.

Planning foresees and forestalls problems. As we plan we say: "Hey, we never thought about this. We're going to have to deal with it next year." So we begin right then to think about how to deal with that possible problem.

Planning defines desired objectives. That should be very clear in your mind.

Planning anticipates and defines the needed means. Usually the budget redefines the plan, but not always. It could be space; it could be people. *Resources* is the key word here, but that should not throw us. The important thing is that *the plan precedes the budget.* We don't start out with the budget and then make the plan on the basis of how much money we have. Yes, a lot of organizations do that, but it represents poor financial practice. *Ministry planning must precede budget planning.* It may have to be revised on the basis of budget planning, but it doesn't start there.

Planning sustains confidence and enthusiasm if you do it well. It provides practical measures of achievement. You can actually see your accomplishment, and that encourages you to do more. Good planning leads to more and better planning.

Planning makes leadership more productive in several ways. The leader constantly playing fireman and rushing from one crisis to another does not plan and therefore will spend his or her life rushing from one crisis to another.

Finally, *planning carries over into spiritual enrichment* because we are able to see the big picture. We see how it is possible for us to plan in a manner that fulfills God's will for our churches and the specific ministries we lead.

The Planning Committee

We have mentioned the planning committee, but let me revisit that. This should probably not be an already existing group of people. For example, a board of deacons or elders would make a poor church planning committee.

You say, "Why would that be the case? We have the most knowledgeable and spiritual leaders of the church on these boards." Yes, but you will almost invariably have one or more elders or deacons who are not forward-thinking people. Highly spiritual people may love Jesus deeply and be very committed to biblical goals for the church but not be able to look beyond tomorrow. Furthermore, deacon and elder boards do not likely represent all the constituents in the church.

I was once indirectly involved with a church that had a self-perpetuating elder board from which no one ever departed. You can imagine the average age of its members after the church had been in existence for thirty or forty years. They were way out of touch with the young people, the young couples, and the families in the church, yet they were making all the decisions. The church went through some gut-wrenching experiences to change that.

The best planning committee selects members from various constituent groups (we earlier called them "stakeholders") in your ministry. If you are the director of a children's ministry program, you will probably want to set up a planning committee that includes a few parents, several children's teachers, a member of the board of Christian education or a Christian education pastor, and possibly a deacon or an elder. It is not necessary for a senior or associate pastor to be on church or ministry planning committees. Often, I suppose, they would be on them, but I don't consider it essential. In a large, multi-staff church, perhaps an associate pastor would be more available for committees than the senior pastor. Obviously, you always keep the pastors informed, but they need not be members of the planning team.

The planning committee for a church or a specific ministry program should consist of a group of forward-thinking people who can examine possibilities, who can think of what the church or ministry might become. The church I attend now has just made some major changes. For years it has been a senior church, with few people under the age of fifty. The average age is probably considerably greater than that. A new pastor came in two years ago and, without breaking everything and tearing the place apart, began to slowly and carefully design new ways to minister to a wider group of people.

One of those ways was to turn one of the rooms (it happened to be the board room) into a nursery. You ask, "Why does a senior church need a nursery?" If we try to bring in families, we need the resources available so that when someone comes with a baby we can say, "Oh yes, glad you brought your baby. We have a new and clean nursery, and somebody staffs it every week." Do we have babies in the nursery every week? No. We look forward to the time when our church is no longer a senior church but a family church, with multiple age groups. We want more people in their forties, thirties, and twenties to attend, so we have taken steps to achieve such a goal.

I have said repeatedly that planning is inseparably related to goals and objectives. Too many leaders don't catch that. They see setting goals and objectives as one of their tasks and planning as another. They see the tasks; they just fail to see that these Siamese twins should never be severed. The closer they remain, the better, because you can't plan without goals, and a goal needs a plan to make it work.

Some people hesitate to talk about "a plan" because such language implies that once we have a document in writing, it dare not be changed; but planning is almost always a *process*. We learn things along the way that force us to change some aspect of the plan. So maybe we should use the old gerund "planning" rather than "plan."

One writer suggests that you prepare a three-year plan and make the third year of each plan the first year of the next plan. So you always have an ongoing process. I like that. It sounds like a good idea. You cannot prepare a one-year plan and consider that you have done your long-range planning. Good planning always generates more planning, whether you do it for one year or three. Ultimately you need to increase the advance time, perhaps from one, to three, to five years.

You probably have many questions about this area if you have not done long-range planning before. Check the further resources in the bibliography for help in this. You will also want to teach planning to new leaders. That will help them and demonstrate to you that you have learned the principles. Don't forget to employ the mission, objectives, goals, and action steps model as you develop new leaders over the next several years.

Wrap-Up

Planning is one leadership skill for which you must first master the principles. Please be careful not to take the early part of this chapter lightly. Models, committees, and the planning process are all important, but the principles provide the glue that holds the whole thing together.

Digging Deeper

1. How would you define planning?

2. What does it mean to say that "planning is cyclically based on evaluation"?

3. What planning pitfalls do you commonly see? How might these be avoided?

4. Briefly explain the Steps in Planning diagram to another person.

5. If you do not already know, explore how your church or organization carries out its planning.

CREATING A CLIMATE FOR DEVELOPING LEADERSHIP TEAMS

"And the things that you have heard from me among many witnesses, commit these to faithful men who will be able to teach others also." (2 Tim. 2:2, NKJV)

6

When you go to a theater, you see many different things on the screen; but around the screen hang those velvet curtains always in view, though you might not see them in the dark. No matter what the movie, however the scenes change, the curtains surround them. They remind me of the climate, the environment in which life happens. A leadership development climate begins with certain principles of ministry. I need to tell you this is *my* list. Your list may be completely or at least partially different. I'm not suggesting this represents *the* list.

Biblical Principles of Ministry

The *New Testament teaches plurality of leadership,* not one single leader who tells everybody what to do, coming down the mountain with the tables of stone. No Elijah, standing by the altar calling down the fire, but a plurality of leadership. Call them what you will—deacons, elders, presbyters. Denominations have different terminology, but all the terms imply a plurality of leadership.

Biblical leadership shuns autocracy. I made that very clear in the first chapter. If you need to go back for review, please do.

Leaders rule by caring and feeding. We gain a clearer picture of leadership by looking at how the term *elder* is used in Scripture. Too many churches view elders as the people who huddle together behind locked doors to make decisions and then come out to tell them what to do. There is a certain ambiance about the noun form in the Greek text of the New Testament that conveys elder *rule.* However, when you follow through on the verb form for *elder,* you find that it deals almost exclusively with caring, feeding, and shepherding. In my opinion, that is what elders do. Whether or not you are an actual pastor or church elder, you can still pick up the principle here and apply it to your own leadership role.

Church leaders are to be recognizable, responsible, and reciprocally accountable. Recognizable—you ought to know one when you see one.

Multiple texts in the New Testament say that people should not be appointed to serve in a church office unless others in the *community* have acknowledged their honesty, not just people in the *church* (see 1 Tim. 3:7). God gives unsaved people the right to make judgments about the mark of the Christian (John 13:35). *Responsible*—of all people who ought to be responsible in an irresponsible society it would be church leaders. And then *reciprocally accountable*, meaning, of course, to each other. They are reciprocally accountable to the congregation, yes, but they are reciprocally accountable to one another first.

God speaks to His people, not just His leaders. I do not believe a pastor or a ministry leader should make major decisions without the involvement of a leadership team. The Holy Spirit lives within every believer. No New Testament evidence tells us that God speaks only to prophets, priests, and kings.

The leader is primarily a coach. A football coach builds a team around him: a defensive coordinator, an offensive coordinator, a quarterback coach, and a special teams coach, and they advise him on what to do. A pastor or other ministry leader needs just as good a team—and one that is just as varied.

Leaders should always focus on ministry, never on money. Do not misunderstand my point here. If you are a pastor, I would never say you should not preach about money. You should preach about money every time you come across a Bible passage that deals with it. But you should not *handle* the money. In my opinion, no pastor should know what individual members of the church give. He should not be counting the money. He should not be writing the checks. He should stay as far away from the money as he can. Pastors have two major vulnerabilities: *adultery* and *misuse of finances.* We see this painfully throughout all the years of the church, particularly in the late twentieth century, and pastors should protect themselves from any temptations in either of those areas.

If you are a program leader or other ministry leader in your church, you should also be careful in situations where money is involved. It would be wise to ensure accountability by setting up policies for the handling of ministry funds.

Ministry is something done by all God's people. Let's not take a good word and make it narrow. *Diakonia* translates into *deacon* but also can mean *service*, and we are all responsible for service. We say we have *ministers* and *laity*, but we created that human division; the Bible does not.

Leaders are not responsible to structure all opportunities for ministry. When Peter and John went to the temple in Acts 3 and saw the lame beggar, that was spontaneous ministry. Ministry is not only something we put into the bulletin, for which we hold training meetings and ask for volunteers. Of course we may do all that for formal ministries, but not for spontaneous ministries.

Leaders must offer biblical answers for current issues. I was scheduled to preach the Sunday the United States military entered Iraq in 2003. Late in the week I had to make major changes in what I would say that Sunday in the middle of a series of messages. Leaders cannot expect people to leap to where we would like them to be; we meet people where they are—physically, spiritually, and mentally.

What Makes a Positive Ministry Climate?

In research carried out by business and industry on the factors contributing to a positive working environment, employees in the secular domain name some items we might not expect. We might assume number one to be *more days off* or *more vacation time*. But they selected *friendly, informal atmosphere.* Can we provide that in the church? A friendly, informal atmosphere? No politics? No fighting? If you think the major task of the church is evangelism and you bring new converts into a church that contains no unity, where people quarrel with one another, you have not done the Kingdom any favors. You cannot develop disciples in that climate.

Conversion is just the beginning. You say, "But it's a question of heaven or hell." Can you name the most important aspect of the church? Can you identify the most important dimension of the "climate" this chapter talks about? *Unity and love.*

People also want *fair and impartial attention to complaints.* If you have created a system whereby people have opportunity to comment on what they don't like, actually do something about what they say. Over the last three months I have become so disgusted with the customer service departments of three different organizations that I wrote them letters. I don't like to do that kind of thing; I don't have time for such nonsense. But I had received some remarkably poor service and wanted to let them know. So I wrote letters to the directors of customer service at the various central home offices. I received no answers from any of the three, so I thought perhaps the letters didn't get through. I sent certified letters to the same people to make sure that they would arrive. Want to know what happened? Nothing. They don't care a hoot about me.

God forbid that anyone should think like that in the church. "Hey, I brought this to the Sunday School Superintendent's attention. I said it's cold in the classroom where I teach on Sunday mornings, and no one has done anything about it. It's just as cold now as it was two years ago." Maybe you cannot change the temperature, but you should not ignore the complaint. Good leaders explain to such people, "We're sorry. Could we find you another classroom? Can we close off the vent in your room and bring in a heater?" You show interest.

And finally *ownership*: We want people involved in more than a job. In fact we don't call ministry a "job" anymore. We should not talk about "workers" anymore. I began ministry in the 1950s when we talked all the time about finding workers for Christian service. It sounded a bit like a queen bee looking for worker bees. Now we talk about "developing team members."

Five Strategies for Developing Team Members

Good leaders don't send soldiers into battle unless they are ready. Every once in a while you have to send someone who is not quite ready. If you coach an NFL team and your number one quarterback is already injured with a broken arm, you play your number two quarterback. If your number two quarterback separates his shoulder at the end of the second half, you have to put in your number three quarterback. Is he ready? No. He has not taken any "snaps," as they say, all week. He usually walks around with a clipboard keeping the stats. Sometimes you have to use a rookie, but it should never become common practice. Avoid it unless absolutely necessary.

You have read repeatedly, *constantly keep people informed.* It is nearly impossible to over-communicate. *Focus on retention.* Hold on to the good people you have. Do you realize how much easier and less expensive it is to hold on to good people in any kind of organization? It could be IBM, Ford Motor Company, or a church of forty people. Good leaders hold on to good people; they never let good people go (or drive them away) and then try to find different people.

How do you keep good people? *Know where their problems are.* That means you invest time talking to them. We have a questionable record in the church on this point. When pastors make changes, they do it secretively. The search committee from another church comes anonymously. When people see a group of five sinister-looking strangers sitting in the back row of the church one Sunday they think, *That's a search committee from another church. We're in trouble. We're going to lose our pastor.* Or the pastor takes a Sunday off and goes to preach somewhere else. In a few weeks he gets up in the pulpit and announces, "Next month I'm leaving for Connecticut and another church." I consider this a terrible way to make a change. We need to create situations in which people can communicate and be involved right from the first time a problem is mentioned.

As I will say so many times, *make sure people are in the right places*, the places for which God has gifted them and to which God has called them. And using another athletic metaphor, *select the best player in the draft*. Ministries need to be created around the gifts of the people on your team. For example, maybe none of your people are especially gifted at teaching. But you have been so focused on finding teachers for your program that you look only for that. Meanwhile you may let some good people who have gifts in evangelism, music, missions, or organization slide by because of that tunnel vision. Veteran leaders select the best player in the draft and then rebuild the team around him or her. Yes, that is difficult; but it pays off in the long run.

Team Dynamics

Here is a simple explanation for why teams work or don't work. Teams accomplish their purposes when people put aside their own personal preferences for a period of time and learn to work together as a team. Teams do not accomplish their purposes when team members are *focused on personal goals* or when teams face *team conflict*, such as arguments among team members, *neglected priorities* (or wrong priorities), or when individual team members' *skills go unused*. Ineffective teams meet together, but they don't minister together.

Common Myths of Team Leadership

Please be careful how you understand this section. This is adapted from "Making Teams Work at the Top" by J. Katzenbach in *Leader to Leader*,[1] the cutting-edge journal of business and management. I often have trouble with students thinking these are axioms and not myths, so they become completely confused. Number one, it is a myth to say that *the primary leader determines whether a ministry is successful or not*. The primary leader does *not* determine whether a ministry is successful or not.

The primary leader must make all the key decisions. This happens in many churches and ministry programs, but it is a myth. Or, *a team is a team because we call it a team*. Not true. Remember the old Abe Lincoln quote? He supposedly asked reporters, "How many legs would a sheep have if you called a tail a leg?" Somebody immediately said "five," and Lincoln responded, "No. Calling a tail a leg does not make it a leg." Calling a team a team does not make it a team.

If every member is in the right place, teams will emerge. Wrong. Forgive my constant athletic metaphors, but the Pro Bowl is not much fun to watch, nor the NBA All-Star Game, because neither consists of team players. These contests feature superstars, all of whom try to get the best shots or make the best tackles. We see talented individuals but we rarely see team play. A team is not a team because we call it a team. Teamwork is taught. Team ministry is learned. Leadership is learned behavior. There are no born leaders. If you find that hard to believe, read about the disciples in the first four books of the New Testament.

The top team is responsible for fulfilling the ministry mission. No. The top team may be heavily involved in developing the ministry mission, but it is only responsible for making sure other teams throughout the entire ministry are committed to it. *Teamwork at the top will lead the team performance throughout the organization.* Sorry, that's not true. Teamwork at the top affords an example. It should serve as a good model, but teamwork is learned.

Teamwork requires many and usually lengthy meetings. Yes, we call meetings. We value the act of convening; but meetings go awry for three reasons. One, we are not clear on the objectives. Two, we have not carefully prepared the agenda. And three, the chairman doesn't take control of the meeting. Fewer, more focused meetings are often much more effective.

Myth eight claims that *winning teams have heavily involved primary leaders.* I would like to talk to Katzenbach about that a bit, but according to his research the answer again is no. Perhaps his research has uncovered the reality that good leaders constantly empower others by trying to "work themselves out of a job."

Number nine, *team members need to spend free time hours socializing with each other.* Sometimes that happens. Many times it does not. In a large city the members of a church staff or ministry team may live a good distance from one another. Socializing with other team members could be very difficult. Sometimes team members are more likely to socialize with people in their neighborhoods or on their jobs than with other people at church.

And finally, *team effectiveness depends upon the right gifts/skills mix.* I would again like to challenge Katzenbach on this. Perhaps we can call this a myth if we add the word "only." It is a myth to say team effectiveness depends *only* on the right gifts/skills mix. The training factor is also a big consideration in team effectiveness.

The Process of Developing New Leaders

Levels of Ministry Leadership

Let's consider the levels of ministry, starting with *the least difficult,* but *not the least important,* levels of leadership. Different levels of leadership require different steps of competence, different growth points of commitment and spiritual maturity. The first is *physical ministry*: taking care of the building or meeting room, locking the doors, moving the chairs, filling the baptistery. Then leaders move up to *program ministry*: setting up programs for children or youth, participating as a program volunteer, serving on the Christian education committee or the music committee. And the highest level is *people ministry*: maybe lay counseling or directly supervising a ministry team. We want to see people grow through the process of these levels, which usually takes several years.

Four Stages in Leadership Development

As we flesh out the idea a little bit more, we can talk about the *convert stage,* where the core values are security and grace, prayer, Bible study, ministry—maybe in that order.

At the second stage people move from convert to *disciple.* The Great Commission does not tell us to make converts; it commands disciple-making. At this stage, security becomes commitment and grace settles into serious discipline. Growing leaders begin reproducing others in prayer and Bible study, and ministry begins to show the early stages of maturity.

The next stage reflects convert/disciple *equipping.* These stages do not take parallel forms, but each stage leads to the next. Equipping means we train people for leadership roles. I set up an elder training program at one church several years ago that was really a two-year mentoring program in which one of the present elders mentored a younger man so that the younger man could attain qualifications for eldership. We offered no guarantee the younger men would become elders when they finished the program, but we worked to develop availability.

And then comes *exercising leadership,* actually taking leadership roles, such as leading a Sunday school class, a boys' or girls' club, or a women's or men's ministry.

The final stage is the *convert/disciple equipping and leadership roles.* So we have come to the place where our learner becomes a leader and we have brought him or her to the stage of ministry leadership. How long does this take? I cannot say. Surely it takes different lengths of time for different people, depending upon where they start. If we can begin with someone eager and already quite mature in spiritual matters, we can make progress quickly in developing such a leader. But if we start with people who have just accepted Christ, we must heed the warnings in the New Testament about putting new converts into ministry leadership positions (1 Tim. 3:6; 5:22). We need people really focused on ministry, people who have their priorities straight: first their relationship to God, second their relationship to their families, third their relationship to the church, and then to their job and everything else in their world.

In closing this chapter let me tell you about my experience as one of the mentoring elders in that program I designed some years ago. I was assigned to a young man in his late twenties, a great guy and a wonderful friend. We played tennis together. He was also a golfer. (I tried golfing with him once, but that was a hopeless endeavor.) Like all the candidates, he willingly said, "I know I am not qualified to be an elder. I understand what the Scripture says. Help me get there." How wonderful to work with that young man, to take him through the skills and experiences for the two years we were together. We still keep in contact. Now, years later, he is still heavily involved in the Lord's work in another city.

But I particularly remember the time he interviewed for another job. An insurance salesman, he decided to change companies. The vice president for personnel of the new company interviewed him, asking all the usual questions. Then he asked, "What is the biggest goal of your life?" Now in a sales situation one would expect the answer they wanted would sound something like, "I want to be your top salesman. I want to be salesman of the year." My friend said to the vice president, "My greatest goal right now is to be thought worthy by my church to be an elder." Imagine the look on that vice president's face when he heard that answer!

Wrap-Up

For years people have been asking me for teaching "tricks," gimmicks and gadgets that capture attention or help solve discipline problems. Many church leaders think the same way about finding and training new leaders. What are the tricks? What are the right words to say? As useful as those questions may be, they are dramatically secondary to the emphasis of this chapter. The kind of environment into which you invite new leaders is much more important than the schemes you use to recruit them, or even to train them.

Digging Deeper

1. Name the kinds of things you think are important in creating a climate for leadership development.

2. What does it mean to "select the best player in the draft"? In what situations do you see this strategy working or not working?

3. Drawing from your experience, name specific ministry tasks that fall under the categories of physical, program, and people matters.

4. Think of a specific ministry setting. Name some practical ways to move a person from a disciple stage to someone who is equipped for serving in that ministry.

5. What three things will you first correct or add to improve the climate of leadership development in your ministry setting?

Notes

[1] Jon R. Katzenbach, "Making Teams Work at the Top," *Leader to Leader* (Winter, 1998): 33–36.

ASSESSING AND RECRUITING LEADERSHIP TEAMS

"Sitting down, Jesus called the Twelve and said, 'If anyone wants to be first, he must be the very last, and servant of all.'" (Mark 9:35)

7

Leaders usually recruit to an existing team that has its own personality and environment. Unless you are a church planter, or starting a new program or ministry, you invite people to join a group of people already in existence. If you need a new Sunday school teacher, that person has to fit in with the Sunday school teachers you already have. When you elect a new deacon, that person must fit with the deacons already serving. That's why climate (chapter 6) is so very important. A leader must first understand the personality and environment of the leadership situation in order to determine how best to assess, recruit, and assign leadership teams.

Think about the difference between a *dependent* congregation and an *interdependent* congregation. Now we have a missing item here—the *independent* congregation. I will not deal with that, but let me at least define it. An independent congregation is one in which the people basically have charge of their church, and leaders come and go. Their attitude is, "Pastor, if you do what we want, and we're comfortable with you, and you meet our needs and satisfy our goals, that's fine; we'll get along great. But don't forget that this is our church." That may represent a minority group of churches, but congregations like that exist, especially in rural areas. But I want to focus on the other two types—the interdependent and dependent congregations.

Dependent and Interdependent Congregations

Remember the leadership styles we talked about as being autocratic, free rein, or team leadership (participatory)? They mirror the three types of churches I just mentioned. To put it another way, an autocratic leader fits nicely with a dependent congregation, a free rein leader with an independent congregation, and a team/participatory leader with an interdependent congregation. So we see that leadership styles are related to congregational styles. There are ministry implications throughout all of this: self-image, programming, financing, staffing, and mission.

Notice the differences. The dependent congregation *looks to the pastor or other key leaders*; the interdependent (which, of course, you can tell by my implications, I would consider more biblical) *looks to each other*. This would be the congregation described at the end of Ephesians 4. The dependent congregation *comes to church*. The interdependent congregation knows how to *be the church*. The dependent congregation shows *concern for program*. The interdependent congregation shows *concern for people*. A dependent congregation focuses on the *building*. An interdependent congregation focuses on the *body*. This is not as neatly boxed as I make it look, but we need some measure in order to see the differences.

I could say much more about that, and Jesus did too in John 4 when the woman of Samaria got caught up in geography. "Our people worship here in Mt. Gerazim. You people worship at Jerusalem. Which is right?" To which Jesus replied, "Forget it. Neither one is at stake here." He did agree that Jerusalem was the correct Old Testament place, but that misses His point. True worship is worship of the heart. God is looking for people who will worship Him in spirit and in truth, people who do not center on the place.

A dependent congregation needs to be *pushed into ministry*, usually by the pastor. The interdependent congregation *creates and initiates ministry—* spontaneous ministry. They look for ministry opportunities. Think again of the biblical example in Acts 3 of Peter and John going to the temple to pray. They were stopped by a lame beggar. From the context, we can assume that this lame beggar had staked out his ground by the Beautiful Gate of the temple; this was his place. They had probably seen him multiple times before. All of a sudden the Holy Spirit stops them. They look at the lame beggar who wants alms. He holds up a little wooden bowl and Peter says, "We don't have any money, but we're going to give you what we do have. In the name of Jesus Christ rise and walk." This was not "Heal a Lame Beggar Week." The Jerusalem Church had not programmed this ministry. Peter and John didn't go to a workshop to learn how to do this. There was no Thursday evening prayer group that met to support it. We should teach people to do spontaneous ministry whenever it occurs, not just what we program at the church.

The dependent congregation takes aim at *problems*. (Think about board, committee, and congregational meetings you have attended. What do they talk about?) An interdependent congregation takes aim at *purposes*. The dependent congregation puts *church in low priority*. They talk as though it holds high priority, but it does not because of the focus on program and building. The interdependent congregation puts *church immediately after God and family*, in third place—not second place. God, family, church, work—in that order. Dependent congregations explain *why things don't work*: "I can't do it because . . . ." An interdependent church *makes things work*.

Don't you love people who make things work? Don't you get frustrated when you go into stores and you have a question, and their only answer is, "I'm sorry, that's not our department." Don't you dislike voicemail—"press one, press two, and press three, and then one again"; finally you get a recorded voice that says, "I did not recognize that answer; you'll have to go back to the main menu." Talk about annoying! I believe that in church ministry, we need to be people with the motto: *We will make things work.*

The dependent congregation stands back to *watch others serve.* The interdependent congregation *eagerly participates wherever there is a need.* They see the need, and they jump in. They have chosen not to be spectators in ministry. And finally the dependent congregation *emphasizes diversity*— not so much how they differ from one another (although that was the problem at Corinth), but how they differ from other congregations. The interdependent congregation has what I like to call a "Kingdom mentality," which emphasizes unity and practices the Kingdom principles outlined in Matthew 18, such as humbling oneself, lovingly confronting sin, and forgiving others.

The personality of your congregation, whether dependent or interdependent, will affect the recruiting strategy you use and the approach you take in setting up leadership teams for your ministry. Obviously, you will have more work to do if you are a part of a dependent congregation. Interdependent congregations are fertile ground for the recruitment process since members are already in the mindset of service. You want to do everything you can to create an environment of interdependence on your ministry team.

Five Fundamental Leadership Practices

In this book I have often referred to leadership specialists Kouzes and Posner. Here is the "Kouzes and Posner Five"—*The Leadership Challenge.* There are five crucial points: Leaders challenge the process. Leaders inspire a shared vision. Leaders enable others to act. Leaders model the way. Leaders encourage the heart.[1] I could quote this for you every morning of your life, and it would not waste your time. This is one of the best lists of leadership behavior that exists anywhere. Let me quickly review what they mean.

Leaders challenge the process does not mean rebellion. It constantly asks the question, "Is there a better way to do this? Is there a better way to organize our Sunday school? Is there a better way to welcome and connect with visitors? Is there a better way to reach unchurched youth? Is there a better way to share the Gospel with our children? Is there a better way to raise money for missions?" On and on the list goes.

Leaders inspire a shared vision. The key word is *shared.* Good leaders do not bring their vision for ministry and expect others to "buy in." Leaders inspire a *shared* vision. Keep this in mind as you invite new volunteers to join your ministry team.

Leaders enable others to act. We call this empowering or facilitation. Leaders make it possible for other people to serve. Quite simply, leaders make it possible for others to lead.

Leaders model the way. This describes mentoring rather than discipling. We too often confuse mentoring and discipling. Mentoring is a general term that has more to do with modeling than it does with teaching spiritual growth. I am not convinced that discipling is always a one-on-one relationship. We have made it that in recent decades. But as you look at the New Testament you see discipling taking place almost always in small groups. How much time did Jesus spend with individual disciples? Peter a couple of times, James and John together. But we have very little evidence in the Gospels that Jesus spent much time with individual disciples. He may have done so. But basically discipling was a group activity. Mentoring describes a lifestyle that helps other people see what to do. When your people lead meetings, they will do it better if they sit in meetings that you lead well. They will pick up those points.

And then *leaders encourage the heart.* Heart attitude is obviously crucial in ministry. Somehow God directed Kouzes and Posner to this wonderful point that is so biblical.

Selecting New Leaders

Assessment of potential leaders must come first. Recruitment *follows* assessment. God guides leaders to select certain people for ministry positions; He helps us through the Holy Spirit to assess those potential leaders (by evaluating readiness and fitness); He assists us in asking those specific people for specific ministries for a specific length of time.

What to Look for in New Leaders

Let's just run down this list:

♦   Christlikeness: becoming more like Christ each year in one's attitudes, words, and actions

♦   Character: who a person is when nobody is watching

♦   Competence: the ability to do the task

♦   Charisma: not someone always on stage screaming, but someone with an outgoing, friendly personality

- Communication skills: someone who can explain things and can write legibly

- Compatibility with existing team members: I consider this crucial. I dislike surprising existing team members with a new player who will not fit.

- Coachability: staying with the team metaphor, however good she is, we want her to get better

- Commitment: to our church, to other team members, to this particular ministry

Common Errors in Selecting New Leaders

When you select new leaders, what are the pitfalls you're likely to find on that dangerous highway?

The first is called *availability bias*. Availability bias means grabbing anyone close. A youth choir director leaves, and we don't want to go through several months of searching for a replacement. So someone says, "Hey, Janice teaches piano lessons; let's make her the choir director." Never mind that she has never led a choir; never mind that she's never taken vocal lessons. She's here; she's available; let's grab her. That's a bad idea—a pitfall in the road of leadership development.

The second is *association bias*, selecting someone already associated with us, a person who is part of our in-group. From this problem comes the nepotism in which a pastor is succeeded by his son in a church. Could that possibly be God's will? Of course, but not likely. That pattern looks more like a family business. When leadership is automatically passed on to the founder's son, we have reverted to an Old Covenant mentality.

And then there is the detour of *agreement bias*, finding someone who agrees with you. Here's another axiom: *Lead to your strength; staff to your weakness.* You do what you do well and find someone else to do what you don't do well, because you don't do everything well. If you recruit another person for a staff or volunteer position who thinks exactly like you, the ministry is no further ahead! You may have less work to do, but there are no fresh ideas, no examples of new thinking, and that is not something you want.

You might ask, "How do you know when new leaders are ready for appointment?" I like to say that new leaders are not ready until I see *meekness*. Also, I want to see *maturity*. I'm assuming that they are maturing and there will be greater maturity later, but I certainly don't want to see a lack of maturity. Finally, I'd like to see some kind of *mentoring*. Has this candidate worked with another more experienced, more dependable, probably older person along the way? There's a great deal to be said for someone spending time serving alongside a mentor figure rather than stepping immediately into a new position.

Basic Guidelines in Recruitment

Match persons and positions. Put people in the right places. It's easy to assume something is the matter with people, when really the people are just in the wrong places. Organizations, including churches, have a terrible habit of putting people in the wrong place and then complaining because they perform poorly.

Follow proven procedures such as prayerful, personal invitation. When you approach people for ministry, *specify persons, tasks, and time.* No universal appeals. Never stand up in front during a church service and say, "We need three new female small group leaders. Please talk to the Small Groups Coordinator in the lobby after the service." When you do that, two bad things could happen. First, nobody might come, and as the poor coordinator stands alone, it becomes obvious to everyone who walks through the lobby that no one wants to lead a small group. Second, someone completely unqualified could walk up to the coordinator and say, "Hey, I heard the announcement. I'd like to lead a small group." What does the coordinator say? "Well, we didn't mean you; we want people who have experience teaching and facilitating group Bible studies!" Please do not do it that way.

Go personally to individuals. Talk about the specific ministry and the length of time this person would be involved. Usually it's good to ask for a year, although it is becoming increasingly difficult in some churches to get people to commit to a year of any kind of ministry. And then finally, *detail the responsibilities and duties.* We call this a ministry description.

Four Keys to Leadership Recruitment

Every recruitment strategy should have four key components. First, *expect ministry involvement.* As a leader you should enter recruiting situations with the assumption that people will say yes. I can hear you now! "Wait a minute. I've been doing this for ten years, and eight out of ten people tell me no." If you develop that mindset, it will pollute the air around your recruiting process. Expect ministry involvement. Expect it from the pulpit. Expect it as a Sunday school superintendent or as a youth director looking for youth sponsors. Be surprised when people say no. "What? You don't want to teach Sunday school? You're passing up this opportunity to communicate the Scriptures to fourth graders? That's amazing. Just amazing." Expect ministry involvement.

Next, *elevate ministry involvement.* Always talk about it in positive terms, never as a dilemma. Here we have yet another leadership axiom. Never say, "You're the last person on my list. Please don't turn me down. You owe me a favor." If you get into that mode, you're in big trouble. People tend to perform at the level at which they were recruited. If you recruit people for a crisis, they will perform as though they have agreed to help out in a short-term crisis, and plan to get out as soon as possible.

Third, *explain ministry involvement.* Remember to be upfront about what the ministry involves and the time commitment it requires. Volunteers don't want to be surprised about these things! Be sure to have a written ministry description that details the specific responsibilities and duties.

And then *evaluate ministry involvement.* I would guess that nine out of ten churches refuse to take this step. They just want willing people. They smile delightedly when someone says, "Yes, I'll do it." Then they close the door and forget it. *We've got a warm body in that junior high class.* Listen. As a leader, you are responsible to evaluate; I emphasize this with all the force at my command. Furthermore, consider yourself warned with yet one more leadership axiom: *In the long run, willingness drives out competence!* If you settle for people who are only willing but basically incompetent, truly competent people will not want to be a part of that ministry.

Activating Leadership Potential

We've been talking about putting people in the right place, and here's my favorite model on that.

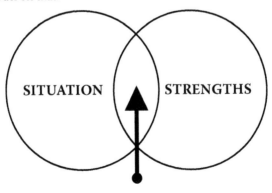

LEADERSHIP POTENTIAL

Leadership potential is activated whenever a person's strengths overlap with the needs of a given situation.

On this diagram, we look first at the little explanation on the bottom: "Leadership potential is activated whenever a person's strengths overlap with the needs of a given situation." *This is not a survival model. This is a thriving model.* "Strength" means spiritual gift, experience, ability to do the ministry task. "Situation" would be the ministry to which you are inviting the person. If a teacher has no ability to teach, no experience in teaching, no gift in this area, you can put that teacher into a class, and he or she may stay there for years, but there is no leadership potential. The more these circles overlap, the larger the center section becomes and the more leadership potential you have. You cannot create leadership development unless you put people in the right place.

Wrap-Up

What kind of personality is your church—dependent or interdependent? This is a key factor in the recruiting process. What are you looking for in new leaders? Remember, recruitment is more than just finding warm bodies. What are the best ways to recruit? Following the principles of this chapter should elevate your percentage of positive responses in recruiting, increase the quality of people on your ministry teams, and help you retain those good people for longer periods of service.

Digging Deeper

1. In one paragraph of no longer than half of a page, write your understanding of the difference between an interdependent congregation and a dependent congregation.

2. Memorize the five leadership principles put forth by Kouzes and Posner. Which principle is most meaningful to you? Why?

3. What leadership selection pitfalls do you see occurring most frequently? What are the dangers in these practices?

4. What does it mean to "match persons and positions"? Why is this important?

5. Explain the idea that "in the long run, willingness drives out competence."

Notes

[1] James M. Kouzes and Barry Z. Posner, *The Leadership Challenge* (San Francisco: Jossey-Bass, 1995).

PREPARING AND PLACING LEADERSHIP TEAMS

"A student is not above his teacher, but everyone who is fully trained will be like his teacher." (Luke 6:40)

8

This chapter logically and necessarily follows the last. Preparing (or training) and placing people depends upon assessing and recruiting, which, in turn, depends on the climate for leadership. This way of thinking about leadership (to which I subscribe) claims that the climate is more important than the timing or technique. I am often asked by churches, "When is the *best time* to prepare people for leadership in ministry posts?" or, "What is the *best way* to do it?" Thirty years ago we had answers to those questions: you do it on Sunday evening before the evening service, using your denomination's materials, materials from a training organization, or perhaps a publisher's helps.

Today the only answer one can really give is, "Whatever works best for you," because churches are so different. But climate remains the issue. As I asked earlier, "To what kind of team and to what kind of leadership environment will you invite these people whom you are preparing for ministry?" Clearly this book commends a team leadership approach characterized by group decision-making and collective responsibility for the outcome of the ministry.

Decentralized Institutional Philosophy

Decision-making and authority in an organization are like hot air. They tend to rise unless you do something to keep them down. To put it another way, unless you deliberately design yourself to be a decentralized team leader, people will allow you to make decisions for them and you will not develop other leaders and will probably end up micro-managing.

Autocratic leadership also minimizes emphasis on biblical qualities. I have a theory that people get the leadership they deserve. For example, the Bible is very specific about qualifications for elders and deacons; you'll find them in 1 Timothy 3. Yet many churches pay no attention to them. They read in the constitution and by-laws that they need seven deacons, and so they elect seven deacons, even though only four qualify to be deacons. That violates our idea of accepting a biblical climate of leadership and developing leaders accordingly. I recommend that you pay very careful attention to the issue of climate.

The Service Triangle

CHURCH EXISTING TO SUPPORT
THE STAFF'S MINISTRY

Bruce P. Powers, ed., *Church Administration Handbook*
(Nashville: Broadman Press, 1985), 309. Used by permission.

These two diagrams go together, and they come from one of Bruce Powers' books, *Church Administration Handbook*.[1] This is a great idea. He first describes the *traditional* triangle of church operation, in which the church exists to support the staff's ministry. Note the general church body at the bottom holding everything up. This foundation elects lay leaders—deacons, elders, program directors, Sunday school teachers—and then on

STAFF'S MINISTRY EXISTING
TO SUPPORT THE CHURCH

Bruce P. Powers, ed., *Church Administration Handbook*
(Nashville: Broadman Press, 1985), 309. Used by permission.

the top we find the staff. "Staff" might mean one pastor, three pastors, or a large paid staff. The question we must ask is whether professional staff members prepare and place people to serve them or design a plan whereby staff members and other leaders serve the people.

Powers argues we need to invert the triangle so we see it is the role of the staff to serve and train other leaders; then those leaders serve and train the general church body for ministry. That follows the biblical pattern. Pastors are ministry facilitators (Eph. 4:11–16). That passage is so important I will include it in the text right here. Speaking about the risen Lord Paul says,

> *It was he who gave some to be apostles, some to be prophets, some to be evangelists, and some to be pastors and teachers, to prepare God's people for works of service, so that the body of Christ might be built up until we all reach unity in the faith and in the knowledge of the Son of God and become mature, attaining to the whole measure of the fullness of Christ. Then we will no longer be infants, tossed back and forth by the waves, and blown here and there by every wind of teaching and by the cunning craftiness of men in their deceitful scheming. Instead, speaking the truth in love, we will in all things grow up into him who is the Head, that is, Christ. From him the whole body, joined and held together by every supporting ligament, grows and builds itself up in love, as each part does its work.*

I know pastors who interpret this passage differently, or at least practice it differently. They would argue that the pastor alone must grow and build up the body. No matter how many people the congregation contains, "It's my church; it's my job; I'm the shepherd, and I take care of the sheep." The Scripture tells us that this holds true in relation to certain sheep, but there are great portions of the flock helped by others—"sheep dogs" or associate shepherds. What an important role for leaders in the middle category! These are lay leaders, not paid staff. Paid staff appear on the bottom of this inverted triangle. Paid staff members support the elected or appointed lay leaders, who in turn serve, direct, and train the general church body. This inverted triangle diagram is important to keep in mind as you create a biblical climate for preparing leaders.

Principles of an Effective Team

An effective ministry team:

1. *Has a clear understanding of its purposes and goals.* It knows what it is supposed to do.

2. *Is flexible in selecting its procedures as it works toward its goals.* It understands that though goals might not change, the procedures by which they reach the goals might change. And its members are not upset when the process changes, because they understand that sometimes that's what has to happen to achieve the product.

3. *Has achieved a high degree of communication and understanding among its members.* We talked about communication before. It's crucial.

4. *Is able to initiate and carry on effective decision-making, carefully considering minority viewpoints.* "Minority" here has nothing to do with gender or ethnicity, but with people who are in the minority viewpoint on some subject. We're right back to product and process. Yes, leaders have to achieve the product, but they must also pay careful attention to the process along the way. Good leaders take care of their people; they do not break the bruised reed. They care for it. Number 5 below says essentially the same thing in a little different way.

5. *Achieves a good balance between productivity and the satisfaction of individual needs.* Process means how people feel about the group. Do people want to be in the group? Are present members satisfied with the way it is led?

6. *Provides for sharing of leadership responsibilities by team members.* Too many team leaders try to do too much by themselves. Good leaders are like good quarterbacks; they set up a play, hand off, throw a pass, but only occasionally run the ball.

7. *Has a high degree of cohesiveness, meaning togetherness and attractiveness, for the members.* They want to belong to each other; they feel that they belong to each other but not to the point of stifling individual freedom. Team ministry is not communism; you don't surrender all your individual rights when you become part of this group. To the contrary, you willingly submit yourself to the best interests of the team, while at the same time offering your own ideas to the team, making available your unique gifts and skills and experience. Yet you can detach yourself from your ideas and suggestions so you do not think people attack you when they challenge your ideas.

8. *Makes intelligent use of the differing abilities of its members.* I know some team leaders who have no idea what their members can do, much less use their gifts and abilities. Knowing your people, plugging them in, and getting the right ones to do the right things are all crucial to team achievement.

9. *Is not dominated by its leader or by any of its members.* Have you ever seen a meeting out of control? Either the chairperson did all the talking and didn't let anyone else speak, or some other high-powered person in the group took over and the chairperson didn't know how to control the group. If you take on a leadership role, you will sooner or later chair team meetings, committee meetings, or board meetings. In that role you must protect weak team members and restrain strong team members so they don't dominate the discussion and the decisions of the group. You do not just want a team; you want an effective team.

10. *Can be objective about reviewing its own process.* A good team does not need someone constantly looking over its collective shoulder to critique its effectiveness. As it develops, part of the learning curve becomes self-evaluation.

The Interlocking Needs of a Team

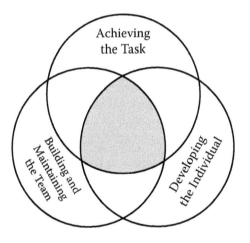

ADAIR'S INTERLOCKING NEEDS OF A TEAM

David Cormack, *Team Spirit* (Grand Rapids:
Zondervan, 1989), 98. Used by permission.

Adair talks about the core responsibilities of a team leader, and this diagram shows "the interlocking needs of a team."[2] We know about the *task,* the *team,* and the *individual.* As always in this type of diagram, the more you push the circles together, the better. Specific tasks, clear goals, reasonable standards, adequate resources, complementary roles among the members of the team all help individual leaders. You exercise acceptance and give that person a sense of value. You help him or her know the expectations; you pay attention to the individual; but at the same time, you build the team with a common purpose, a supportive climate, a sense of group achievement, and a common identity. You want to be the kind of leader who can give adequate attention to all three circles.

How Team Leaders Facilitate Involvement

The word *facilitate* means that you make possible what these people do; you make their roles easier and more productive. This describes the function of a college dean. He or she almost always gives up some teaching responsibility, perhaps all teaching responsibility, so that others can teach better. He or she makes teaching possible and effective. No college needs a dean if there are no faculty, and it needs no faculty if there are no students. Each group *facilitates* the other.

Below are some ways leaders can facilitate involvement:

♦ *Leaders think positively.* They believe people are capable of using their freedom to serve and enhance the ministry organization. Good leaders show optimism about the people they picked, prepared, and placed. They believe people can and will use their freedom—not just their minds, bodies, or the instruction we give them—to serve and enhance a ministry organization.

♦ *They value the act of convening as a primary part of their role.* Stop apologizing for committee meetings; stop apologizing for getting people together. Convening is part of a team leader's role—bringing people together. A committee meeting is as much ministry as the event the committee meeting plans! But people rarely see that. Good leaders convene *well*; they do not have two-, three-, and four-hour meetings that accomplish little. I am a proponent of the one-hour meeting. I can't always do it; I don't bat 100 percent; but I have disciplined myself to conduct one-hour meetings. The key is to handle most things by small groups and sub-committees before the main meeting begins.

♦ *They learn how to design a meeting for group decision-making.* Leaders (chairpersons) can structure the agenda and terminology to allow the group to make decisions. You look for consensus. Take a vote if you must. Consensus and voting are two different acts, but they are not necessarily inconsistent. More on that in chapter 12.

◆ *They decentralize themselves repeatedly.* Decentralize yourself; don't let people make you the big dog, the commander-in-chief, the chief executive officer. In ministry decisions, you may have different responsibilities, but you always take the yoke and share the burden. Sharing the burden does not mean that everyone who comes to you is entitled to the solution to a particular problem. In fact, if you take over another person's problems and give her solutions, two negative things can happen: (1) What you told her may work. So now she comes back to you every time she has a problem because you keep telling her the answer. The result is that she will never become a leader. (2) What you told her may not work. Obviously the fault is yours because it was your idea. She need not take responsibility, and people who avoid responsibility never become leaders. You cannot facilitate leadership development by solving other people's problems for them.

◆ *They form lateral partnerships.* In organization theory we talk about line relationships and staff relationships. Line relationships are vertical—who is responsible to whom and who is responsible for whom. Staff relationships are horizontal. In a college most vice presidents are in lateral relationships, so they must learn to relate to one another on an equal plane. Ministry leaders must also build horizontal relationships with people on their team.

How People Best Learn Leadership

If you are seriously interested in developing leaders, you need to know how that is best done. The following list comes from Ken Callahan's book *Effective Church Leadership*, but the interpretation and application are mine.[3]

◆ *People best learn leadership in an environment of* objectives, *not* activities. We must expect them to achieve specific goals, not just be active and busy. Productivity, not activity, is the key.

◆ *People best learn leadership in an environment with a high delegation of* authority, *not* responsibilities. Authority must be balanced with competence. We do not give people tasks they cannot handle, because that will frustrate them. But when they attain competence to handle greater responsibility and we don't give it to them, that frustrates them as well. Eventually, either error will lose good people to the ministry.

◆ *People best learn leadership in an environment where decision-making is participatory and straight forward;* the biggest decisions made by the most people and the smallest decisions made by the least amount of people, or those who are closest to the actual situation. Just think of a church that plans to build an expensive new building. This decision cannot be made by the pastor or the pastoral staff alone; it must be determined by as many people as possible, probably a congregational vote, depending on how the church's constitution is written.

But suppose a church needs to spend $50 to replace some shrubs that died over the winter. This is not a decision for a congregational vote. Instead, one or two people who are responsible for building maintenance should make that decision. People working in the trenches, such as Sunday school superintendents, club program leaders, youth directors or sponsors, should be empowered to make the decisions close to them.

♦ *People best learn leadership in an environment of* continuity, *not* discontinuity. Continuity means that one needs time to learn leadership; one needs familiarity; one needs to be in a situation in which procedures are predictable. New leaders need ministry control, and that takes time, as we have already discussed. They need to understand objectives and experience the fulfillment of objectives. When you're in a discontinuous situation, it is very hard to do that.

One of my former students went to a church in Colorado as an assistant pastor. In six years he served under four or five different pastors! They walked through like tourists. Amazingly he survived all of that. But he didn't learn leadership while he was there; he learned survival. Those two behaviors are not the same thing.

♦ *People best learn leadership in an environment of* competence, *not* willingness. As we have discussed, people who are really competent will not want to participate in a ministry in which the only requirement is willingness.

Suppose you have a bad church choir and a couple moves to town and visits your church. She was a soprano with an opera company in some major city. When she hears your choir, what is her first thought? "I need to get up there and help that choir get better"? I don't think so! I think she leans over to her husband and tells him, "Please don't tell anyone here that I sing. I wouldn't be caught dead up there with that choir."

I hear you say, "Well, she shouldn't think that way." If you want to lead in a world of *shoulds* and *oughts* and *woulds*, you had better forget ministry, because most churches do not offer that world. We deal with reality, with the way people think and act, not the way we expect them to behave.

♦ *People best learn leadership in an environment of* local development, *not* centralized development. Local may refer to a single congregation or ministry program doing the training instead of a denomination. The key is to learn as close to the job as possible. Developing leaders should go to Sunday school conventions or spiritual formation conferences; the workshops are helpful and the principles are great. But there is nothing like being mentored and developed by someone where you'll be serving.

Understanding Power and Influence

Organization authority (power) comes from *control over valued resources.* Where does that control originate? From *visibility.* After seminary, my son was hired as a Pastor of Christian Education. The church discovered he had previously led music in a church, so they made him Associate Pastor of Christian Education and Music. A Pastor of Christian Education can get lost. He or she is always off helping someone. Many people may not even know their Christian Education pastor. But when you are on the platform every Sunday leading every congregational song, you become very visible. Visibility gives influence.

Talent and ability are also valued resources. If you are the only person in the church who can play the piano, and you get angry at the pastor and don't come for three weeks, this creates a big problem. Soon somebody will knock at your door saying, "Please come back." *Money* obviously is a valued resource; the treasurer is an influential person, and so is the wealthy donor. *Relationships* bring influence. Friendly people and older people usually have influence and authority because they have built relationships. Finally, *knowledge* is an influence source. People who know certain things tend to have influence. A lawyer, a builder, an accountant might be useful.

Let's end this chapter with another leadership axiom: *You empower other people by giving them some of your power.* That's what makes leadership possible. You ought to be constantly empowering other leaders. Remember the action verbs in the previous chapter and this one: Assess, Recruit, Prepare, and Place.

Wrap-Up

The climate you create is more important than the timing and the techniques in preparing people for ministry. Have you decentralized ministry decision-making? Have you sought to create a biblical climate where staff and lay leaders serve the general church body? Preparing people for ministry depends on building an effective team that is focused, flexible, balanced, and high in member involvement and sharing. Don't forget that people learn leadership best by spending time in a competent and empowering environment.

Digging Deeper

1. Find all the leadership "axioms" in this chapter. Pick a few of them to reflect upon and apply to your own leadership role.

2. Explain a "decentralized leadership philosophy" in the context of ministry.

3. Without checking the chapter, identify in your own words five ways people best learn leadership.

4. Write on a sheet of paper three leadership behaviors you will change or adopt as a result of having studied this chapter.

5. Describe to someone (maybe a classmate) Adair's "Interlocking Needs of a Team."

Notes

[1] Bruce P. Powers, ed., *Church Administration Handbook* (Nashville: Broadman Press, 1985), 309.

[2] This diagram is found in David Cormack, *Team Spirit: A Management Handbook* (Grand Rapids: Zondervan, 1989), 98.

[3] Kennon L. Callahan, *Effective Church Leadership* (San Francisco: Harper & Row, 1990), 165.

CHALLENGING AND
CHANGING NEW LEADERS

*"Because they do not change, therefore
they do not fear God." (Ps. 55:19b)*

9

Let's start by picturing a mountain climber, reminding us that the process of change moves forward by short steps. Let me emphasize again that the climate makes the difference—not the icy mountain and the climber with the spiked shoes, but the environment in which you want to produce change. Many experts consider it the most important factor in the change process.

When you take a new leadership position, try not to change anything major in the first year. Remember my point about not having ministry control for a year? You don't want to change anything major *unless* (and here's the exception) you have been chosen as a change agent. The Board of Trustees at a small Christian college told me (after I had arrived on the scene and signed a five-year contract to be president) that if I had not agreed to come they were going to close the school. As you can imagine, I faced major changes from day one, and we made some huge changes in the first year. But that is not the way I like to lead. Nor is it the way anyone should like to lead, but I was hired as a change agent, and that constitutes the exception to moving forward slowly.

Change—Learning to Use Restraint

First, restraint is necessary because *people tell you things they don't mean.* They do not intend to lie; they just tell you what seems culturally correct. In the first year, people offer leaders freedom in the hope they will choose not to use it. "Do anything you want. We are just delighted you came, and we will support anything you want to do."

Second, *you see things that are not there.* Young leaders especially read things into new situations, or situations they have not encountered before. They find readiness for a big project: a new building, a different location for the men's retreat, a contemporary worship service, a new name for the Vacation Bible School program, whatever it might be. As a leader you see things that do not exist because they seem so clearly fixed in your mind; you can't imagine how any sane human being could disagree.

Finally, *you want to change more than you can.* This is also a product of immature leadership. You need to know your tolerance limit, and you need to know the group tolerance limit. You might start out in a change process and see things go well. Since no one complains you think, *This is great. They always told me change would be difficult, but it's not difficult. Everybody is marching in step and this is easy.* Then you get half a mile down the road, and suddenly the army stops. They stop because your tolerance limit for change is probably well beyond the group's limit. In this context, "tolerance limit" means the point at which you get frustrated and the point at which they get frustrated.

How Organizations Confront Change

Organizations can confront change in four different ways. *They hang onto the past.* They say, "It has always worked in the past. This is what we like. This is what we do, and we're going to hold on to it." Or, they *treat change as a threat or a problem to be solved.* Change is not a problem. Proper change brings improvement. But some people see change as a threat or a problem to be solved.

Organizations also *extrapolate from the present to the future,* which means they do the same things, only more of them. If you have any experience as a college student, you have stood (perhaps many times) in a registration line. Registration lines are not necessary. I decided when I became Vice President of Academic Affairs at Dallas Seminary that we would get rid of registration lines. I did not know how we would do it, but I had had my fill as a student and as a faculty member watching students in registration lines. They would wait and wait, only to discover that they were in the wrong line or they did not have the proper financial papers or the class had closed. It took us about two years, but we completely did away with registration day and registration lines. We placed everything online; students could open their computers anywhere to see if a class had closed and to access any other information. We chose not to create larger lines or more lines or to assign more staff to the process but rather to do something completely different.

And that's number four—some organizations embrace change to *create a preferred future.* Strategic planning, as noted in an earlier chapter, means creating a preferred future, designing the future, showing how you will move from the mission to the vision. With a precise mission and a well-designed vision, you move on to plan objectives, goals, and action steps that form a bridge between mission and vision.

Seven Dynamics of Change

Seven is no magic number here; we simply want to review the dynamics of change. As a leader, you need to know these issues, and you must respond to them properly.

At first *people will feel awkward, ill at ease, and self-conscious.* This is normal, and you tell them that. People come to you and say, "I'm just not comfortable with this change," and you respond, "A lot of people aren't comfortable with the change. This is quite common. You're fine. You're normal." Of course, there may be deeper reasons why persons are not comfortable with a specific change, and you need to listen to these. But people who feel nervous about change in general will just need some gentle reassurance.

People initially focus on what they have to give up. They need to express this. We dare not let them carry it around privately in their hearts, maybe grumbling about it with other folks. They need to talk about it—maybe not at a public meeting, but at least to you or perhaps to other leaders. Encourage them to say, "I really feel bad about this. I miss the hymnbooks. I miss being a part of the traditional choir. I miss doing something that we've always done in our church." Other people may feel the change means abandonment of the core beliefs or mission of the church or ministry program. When this happens, you must help them to see that the changes only imply a different, and even more effective, means of accomplishing the mission; the core beliefs and values are still the same.

People feel alone even if everyone goes through the same change. If we change a major feature about the church service, we all experience it; but some people believe that others can handle it better than they can. That makes them feel alone. They assume, "I've been here longer, so I've grown more accustomed to what we've done in the past." Or, "My parents were founders of the church, and they would be very upset about this." Instead of criticizing them and saying, "People just don't like change, and I know that, so I am going to push ahead anyhow," let them know that you understand their struggles. If it's true, tell them that you also struggle. Many leaders have a hard time with change as well. The results are not always everything we would like them to be.

Furthermore, *people can only handle so much change.* Remember, most people do not respond negatively just to change itself. More often we create problems by the way we go about change. We expect change, but the rapidity and volume of change presents the difficulty. Too much change can bring people to a point of paralysis at which they cannot even function properly in ministry. Perhaps they feel uncomfortable—and then they leave.

Please never have the attitude, "Good. One more opponent gone. Now we can really move ahead." That kind of attitude reverses a shepherd's heart.

It does not reflect a New Testament response, which is always redemptive. Biblical leaders do not try to get rid of people—even troublemaking people. Our talk about "backdoor revival" denies redemptive leadership. God will take care of problem people. He certainly handled the Ananias and Sapphira problem with dispatch!

Remember too that *people are at different levels of readiness for change.* What causes this? Experience, not age. We erroneously think that older people will more likely resist change. Try flipping around things in a youth group. Take away certain music they are addicted to and see what happens. You may get more negative reaction against change than senior adults could generate. Never forget that experience provides the key to readiness for change. People who have traveled a great deal, been members of a number of different kinds of churches, maybe even different denominations, or have had wide education are more ready to accept change than people who have never left the farm and have gone to the same church every week of their lives.

People will also be concerned that they don't have enough resources for change, the old bricks-without-straw problem. They might be right. The leaders may have worried about this as well. What do you say? How about, "No, we don't know how we will pay for this, but we think God wants us to go onward in faith, and I believe He will provide the resources." Let's remember in relation to the above six, *if you back off too easily on change, people revert to their old behavior.* That reversion causes a loss of momentum. The real reward of change, no matter how small the change and however well you handle it, is momentum, which leads to new learning on the part of people. When you get discouraged and back away from the project, people revert to their old behavior, and it becomes that much more difficult to try again next time.

Process of Implementing Change

In my book *Feeding and Leading* I attempted to go into great detail on the process of change and the following graphic summarizes those pages.[1] *Determine needed change.* The need is ascertained by evaluation and long-range planning. *Decide on the direction of change.* You achieve this by group decision-making, not by one particular person deciding everything. *Design implementation.* The design is determined by the planning committee we have already talked about in chapter 5. And finally, *declare plans and process.* Here the problems begin.

The *announcement stage* lays the trap. Assume we want to open a daughter church. What will change? Well, we will ask ten families from our church who live on the south side of town to leave our church and, in a missionary effort, become the nucleus of the daughter church.

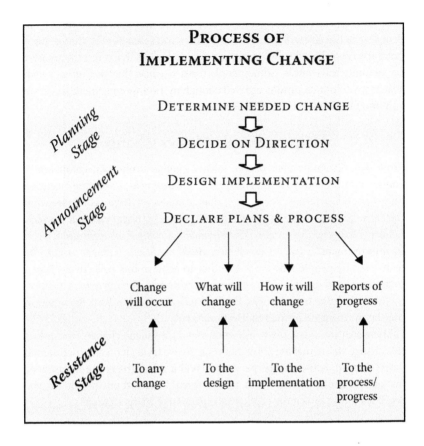

Already, we have problems on our hands. To say that we will start a daughter church will probably not upset many people. But when we describe the location, and say that ten families will likely leave, unless we have prepared this well in advance, such an announcement could be a mine field. People question how this will affect our church. What about the income from these ten families? They will obviously give their gifts to the new church. How will that affect our budget? Will my friends be among those ten families? And will we get ten families here to replace them?

Churches tend to be great at the numbers game. How many people will come? How many dollars will they bring? We do not excel at Kingdom thinking. Perhaps the daughter church on the south side will do more for the work of God than if all these people come to the main building.

Remember that reports of progress are very important. Keep people clearly informed. This falls to the planning team. That is why people must have access to its members all along the way.

In the *resistance stage*, we admit that some people want no change at all. Probably only a few will feel that way. Others will resist not the change itself but the way you handle the change; and, in my opinion, that offers the greatest opportunity for trouble. Some people resist because they *feel uninformed.* When we do not communicate well enough in the announcement stage, we run into problems in the resistance stage.

Helping People Master Change

Three key attributes help people master change—concepts, competence, connections.[2] First, you *tune in to the environment,* assuming accurate information. Don't move forward on change unless you have a good idea what the consequences might be. *Challenge the prevailing organizational wisdom.* Leaders challenge the process. *Communicate a compelling aspiration,* a call to improvement, a call to excellence. *Build coalitions.* Change occurs by team play, by people who work together to achieve this collectively. *Learn to persevere* and to gradually *transfer ownership to a working team.* Coalition members become team leaders. Finally, *make everybody a hero.* Recognition may be the most underused motivational tool.

There are three questions to ask when making a difficult change. First, ask, is this change we are making permanent? Or are we trying it on an experimental basis? Second, is the change pervasive? Will it affect the entire ministry or just one particular aspect? Third, is it personal? Does just one person (maybe you?) want this, or is it the collective conviction of a larger group?

The Base Hit Strategy

This approach to change means big wins from small beginnings. We start by *giving people a sense of choice.* My daughter-in-law practiced this well when her children were younger. She would say, "It's bedtime. Do you want to wear the pink pj's or the blue pj's?" In other words, you *are* going to bed, but you have a choice. What color of pajamas do you wish to wear? Choice becomes the focus.

Don't push people into change. When I became Dean of Dallas Seminary, I did not have an agenda of change. But I thought we ought to change the Th.D. to a Ph.D. The former seems a bit obsolete, but the Ph.D. is the most widely accepted degree in the American educational system. I worried and prayed about this for several months and then went into the August assembly of the Doctoral Committee and said, "Gentlemen, I've really been considering something. I wonder if you would be interested in changing the Th.D. to a Ph.D.?" And they said, "You know, Dean, we've been talking about that for a long time, and we are not sure how to do it." I went in with no intention to push people into change, and I came out with that change virtually an accomplished fact—within that same year it appeared in the catalog. God can make people ready for the right changes!

Reduce everything to its basic essentials. In the academic world, this means, "Will anybody take this course?" Faculty members often come to deans and say things like, "I would like to offer a course in Advanced Ugaritic." Deans respond, "Good idea. I know you did your doctoral dissertation on that, and you are an expert. No one could teach it better than you. I have one question: Who will take this course? If we offer Advanced Ugaritic as an elective, will anybody show up?" Always state the bottom line; get down to the essentials.

Also, *divide tasks into small chunks.* Training new volunteer leaders presents a huge task, and it is very time consuming. Choosing new Sunday school curriculum can be stifling. Long-range planning must be broken into small pieces so it doesn't look so threatening.

Finally, *experiment continuously.* Leaders challenge the process. If you experiment continuously, people will see that change does not threaten them, because it can be reversed. In one church I pastored I wanted to exchange the Sunday evening service for home fellowship meetings. The elders said, "Absolutely not. We're not going to do that." So for two years I waited, brought it up every once in a while, but their apathy lingered. Finally we agreed to try it on a temporary basis for one year. After that year, we never went back.

We close with Thomas Gilmore's model showing four groups of people from both ends of the *power continuum* and both ends of the *favor or oppose continuum.*[3] Notice the four rectangles. The *strong-favorable* describes strong people who favor the change. You need to organize them. People who are *weak and favor the change* need to be empowered. *Strong people opposed* to the change need to be "reframed," or to put it in my own words, you will need to "redefine the issues" with them. And Gilmore proposes we "co-opt" those who are *weak and opposed.* That sounds as though you might take them behind the barn and shoot them, but Gilmore really means that they don't know enough about the issue. They need more communication. Good leaders explain the change process so people have the option to become strong and committed.

Please do not give up on people during the change process because they move too slowly. Since you didn't change anything major in the first year, you have the opportunity to be a redemptive leader. You probably have more than enough support. God forgive you if you make a major ministry change because fifteen people voted for it and fourteen people voted against it. On the other hand, I doubt you will always get twenty-nine unanimous votes.

STRATEGY IMPLICATIONS
FOR STAKEHOLDER TYPES

		ATTITUDE	
		Favor	*Oppose*
POWER	Strong	Organize	Reframe
	Weak	Empower	Co-opt

Thomas N. Gilmore, *Making a Leadership Change*
(San Francisco: Jossey-Bass, 1988), 136. Used by permission.

Wrap-Up

Team leadership works best when a group of people agree to carry out ministry or make some change, and they agree to support it even if they didn't like the idea. That shows spiritual maturity. That makes possible the kind of change that will bring about improvement and lead your ministry to excellence. But remember, don't make changes too soon; don't make too many changes; be very careful how you explain the changes and how you deal with people who seem to be opposed. Change is good when it means improvement. Change for the sake of change has no value at all. But if it enhances God's Kingdom and moves our ministry more toward excellence, then we need to be leaders willing to help other people participate in reasonable aspects of change.

Digging Deeper

1. Name two major axioms of the change process. Explain how they might apply to your present ministry.

2. Why do good leaders use restraint rather than force during a period of change?

3. What is meant by "organizations tend to extrapolate from the present to the future"?

4. As a leader, what do you do or say when people complain about what they have to give up as the result of a change?

5. What happens if you give up too soon during change? Why?

Notes

[1] Kenneth O. Gangel, *Feeding and Leading: A Practical Handbook on Administration in Churches and Church Organizations* (Wheaton: Victor Books, 1989), 151–155.

[2] The information in this paragraph and the following one is adapted from R.M. Kantzer, "The Enduring Skills of Change Leaders," *Leader to Leader*, Summer 1999.

[3] Thomas N. Gilmore, *Making a Leadership Change* (San Francisco: Jossey-Bass, 1988), 136.

SUPERVISING SATISFIED TEAMS

"The God of heaven will give us success.
We his servants will start rebuilding." (Neh. 2:20)

IO

This important dimension of our study will focus on how we continue the development of volunteers from the moment of recruitment on through training and retaining. As an introduction I offer several key words to describe the "climate" I have mentioned so frequently.

Key Words for Biblical Leaders

The first is *Kingdomness.* You need people willing to look at the big picture of God's Kingdom, not just the specific ministry God has led them to do. I have talked to pastors and church program leaders who say, "Yes, I used to spend a lot of time training our volunteer leaders, but then I discovered their companies would transfer them and our church would no longer have the benefit of what we had taught them." This is non-Kingdomness. Such thinking is myopic. If you train someone in your Oklahoma church, and a company moves that person and his family to Chicago where he, his wife, and his children serve God in a church, you have contributed to the Kingdom of God. That is not a loss but a gain. Not a minus but a plus. But only if you take the big picture of Kingdomness.

The second is *meekness.* Common to the life of Jesus, it also appears throughout the ministry of the New Testament apostles. Look at Peter in the Gospels; he doesn't look at all meek. But when he comes back from leading Cornelius to Christ and he's confronted by Judaizing Christians, we see a new Peter (Acts 11). The Judaizers were not the Pharisees and the Sadducees but Christians who were still committed to the traditions of the past. They say, "Where in the world have you been, Peter? We heard you were eating with Gentiles." The old Peter would have whacked off their ears. The new Peter says, "Well fellows, let me just tell you about what happened." He explained again what God did. And they replied, "God did it; we're not going to argue with you about it." Meekness, of course, must never be confused with weakness.

Bodiness is third. Here I use a passage that has meant a great deal in my own life, one that has given me strength and direction in my own ministry. It is found in a very familiar context, but people don't usually read far enough to get to the text. Here is Romans 12 beginning at verse 1:

> *Therefore, I urge you, brothers, in view of God's mercy, to offer your bodies as living sacrifices, holy and pleasing to God—this is your spiritual act of worship. Do not conform any longer to the pattern of this world, but be transformed by the renewing of your mind. Then you will be able to test and approve what God's will is—his good, pleasing and perfect will.*
>
> *For by the grace given me I say to every one of you: Do not think of yourself more highly than you ought, but rather think of yourself with sober judgment, in accordance with the measure of faith God has given you. Just as each of us has one body with many members, and these members do not all have the same function, so in Christ we who are many form one body, and each member belongs to all the others. (vv. 1–5)*

Single-facedness. I've never exactly heard the word put that way, so I may have to neologize. This person says the same thing to everybody. A leader does not make up one story to a person in trouble, another story to her friends, another story to the deacons, and yet another story to the congregation. I have seen this many times. I have heard my supervisors tell me one explanation of an event, and then in a meeting, I listened to them explain the event from a completely different contextual viewpoint and slant it in a different way. Now it's one thing to structure your message differently to be relevant to different audiences, but any hint of dishonesty is unacceptable behavior for Christian leaders. Sometimes you are not in a position to stop others, but certainly you should never do it yourself.

Fairness is very important. At the end of Colossians 3, Paul talks about how slaves should behave. Then at the beginning of chapter 4, in the same context, he talks about masters or owners (employers or leaders) and how the responsibility for leaders is to be fair.

PERFORMANCE EFFECTIVENESS EQUATION

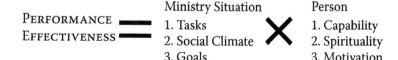

PERFORMANCE EFFECTIVENESS	Ministry Situation	Person
	1. Tasks	1. Capability
	2. Social Climate	2. Spirituality
	3. Goals	3. Motivation

The Performance Effectiveness Equation

Performance effectiveness equals the *ministry situation* times the *person.* What is the ministry situation? Tasks, social climate, and goals. This is a general description of any kind of position: tasks to do, a social climate in which they must be done, and goals to be reached. You may recall that overlapping circle diagram we looked at in chapter 7 about putting people in the right place in order to activate leadership potential. Notice that tasks require capability, the social climate demands spirituality, and the goals must have motivation. Effective leaders are capable of the task, they are spiritual even in a social climate that is not spiritual, and they are motivated to achieve the goals required in their particular situations.

Principles of Supervision

1. *Personal attitudes*—Examine both the new leader's attitude toward other people and toward you, and your attitude toward the person.

2. *Impartiality*—This goes right along with the fairness we talked about earlier.

3. *Clear-cut goals*—We always evaluate according to the objectives and goals that have been previously determined. We do not evaluate on a "gut level" feeling.

4. *Task clarification*—If your leader doesn't know what he is supposed to do, you cannot do an effective evaluation.

5. *Responsibility*—How responsible is this person? Does she take responsibility and practice accountability?

6. Is there *communication* both up and down? Does this leader communicate well enough? Have you communicated well enough about the ministry that he or she is responsible to do?

7. *Ministry control*—Once again, *not* people control but whether or not the person has control of the ministry.

8. Has there been any *training?* Here you basically evaluate yourself. Have you provided training opportunities for this person to grow and develop along the way?

Guidelines for the Evaluation Process

First, *establish a person-centered climate.* Evaluation should not be an impersonal experience. You can't evaluate by sending around a form, having people fill out the form, and then sending back the results. Evaluation must be person-centered.

Second, *examine people in key areas.* Let's take a Sunday school teacher as our example here because it is a ministry with which we all are familiar.

The call. Is this person called? One could argue she never should have been appointed in the first place without evidence of a call. But she could have been appointed before you came and you had nothing to do with it. Or maybe in the past you thought there was a call, but now you discover that she no longer feels called to this particular ministry and therefore needs a change.

Does the person display *dedication* to this ministry? Commitment is seriously loving the people she ministers to and recognizing that God is using her.

Do you see *competence?* Is she getting the ministry task done? Is she doing it well?

Training. Has she gone through some form of training to enable her to carry out this responsibility?

What about *relationships with other people?* Leaders make sure that people serving with them relate well to one another. You cannot have one person causing disunity and disruption in a ministry team.

Productivity may seem the same as competence, but here we are looking at end results; we call them "outcomes." She may be a competent teacher, but are her students learning?

Evaluate with Various Measures

Use a *student questionnaire.* One way to test a teacher's effectiveness is to ask his or her students. If you have been in college or seminary classes, at the end of the semester, you may have filled out a form and the teacher received the collective results of this form. I don't think this should be done anonymously. We want people to be responsible for their critique of others.

Supervisor observation (done by the departmental superintendent or the Sunday school superintendent). Perhaps teacher evaluation can be handled by a full-time paid associate pastor of Christian Education, but probably we want the superintendents to do that. In this case, they are closer to the line of fire.

Self-analysis forms. I have found that self-evaluation is the best kind. I ask people to evaluate themselves using the same form that I use. So I fill out the form on the person, and she fills out the form about herself. Then we get together eyeball to eyeball in a person-centered climate, and we talk about it. Suppose we rate these items on a scale of one to ten; if we both have a seven on question number one then we are probably right. Now we get down to number six, and she thinks she is functioning at nine and I think she deserves a three. Now we have something to talk about. Or if she registered a three and I put down nine, that would be an interesting discussion.

Equip your volunteers for improvement. Evaluation exists for improvement, not to tell them everything they're doing wrong, not to move them around (although that may be the outcome), but to help them improve. One more thing. I believe in complete *mutual* evaluation. Anyone you evaluate should also evaluate you. You would probably need a different form for that, but again you would both fill out the form. I did this as a department chairman, and I did it as vice president. I asked nine department chairmen to evaluate me as their dean and took very seriously what they said.

Keeping Team Members on Track

Leaders always face the task of keeping the team on track. How do we do that? We make sure they know their purpose. I've said this many times, and I'm going to keep saying it: You can't overcommunicate!

Are they doing ministry in the right way? They may be doing the right things, and that's really good, but are they doing them in the right way? Just because effectiveness seems more important than efficiency does not mean efficiency isn't important.

Train them to play their positions. I'll stick with the sports metaphor here. Train them to play their positions so they know what to do in the game.

Show them how to be serious at practice. Picture a high school basketball team that just fools around at practice. Their easy-going coach scrimmages a bit but requires no drills, no shooting free throws, and no discipline. Or imagine a church music team that uses its one-and-a-half–hour practice time on Thursday evenings to catch up on the latest gossip. Every time there is a break between songs or the leader calls certain parts to rehearse, everyone else starts talking. Neither of these groups will be a winning team.

Emphasize decision-making participation. This is an old song that you hear me singing time after time. See chapter 12.

Give them resources for solving problems. Don't solve their problems for them. Provide them with resources. Ask questions: "Have you talked to so and so?" "Have you looked here?" "Have you checked out this book?" "Have you thought about this?"

And then, *consistently widen their perspective.* Make this a lifetime leadership goal, especially working with youth. I do it with adults too, but adults tend to widen their own perspectives. Youth try to fulfill a requirement, finish a project, and live through the experience. When students encounter me they discover I do not have the same idea. The plan is not just to live through the year; the plan is to have as many new and challenging experiences as possible. I often find myself in conversations that sound something like this:

"Tomorrow you will do such and such."
"But no, I can't."
"Yes, you can."
"But I've never done it before."
"Doesn't matter; you're going to do it."

New Motivational Tools

We've seen a lot of good research in recent years on motivational tools. Let me talk about a few of those.

Mission Possible

Help people believe in the importance and value of their tasks. Douglas McGregor came up with "Theory X" and "Theory Y" to explain how leaders think about people. Theory X says people are slow and often stupid. They will shirk the work if you don't watch them all the time. Theory Y says, no, basically if you give people freedom they'll be responsible. If you teach them how to do the job, they'll do it well and be happier.[1]

Flexibility

You've heard about flex-time in work programs. People want more control over their own time and lives. Why not let them choose from a menu of ministry options? Let's not force people into certain places just because we have need of warm bodies there.

Reputation Building

Recognize people for doing a good job (like the MVP trophy). We have to be careful that we do not always recognize the same people, even though they appear to be the best players on the team and consistently make the Pro Bowl year after year. As a good leader, you recognize people for doing a good job even though they may not be gifted enough to go to the Pro Bowl.

Knowledge

"Learning organization" is a great term commonly used for businesses today, and it certainly applies to the church. I believe sound Bible teaching is a major draw even though we are in a period of weak Bible teaching in evangelicalism. Volunteers will be drawn to participate in your ministry if you offer opportunities for advanced Bible learning as part of their training or service.

Achievement

Value creation and ingenuity. Give rewards based on measurable results. Develop people who can say, "We did it! We tackled it together and we did it!"

Keys to Retention

How do we keep good people on the team? Begin with a definite term of service. Use a fair system of promotion and rotation, moving people up into positions of greater responsibility and moving people around into different positions on occasion. Set specific goals so you can evaluate fairly. Provide adequate support. And build in rewards and recognition. Remember— leaders encourage the heart.

The Heartbreak of Releasing People

Let's end with this separation checklist. When you release people, and you do on occasion have to release volunteers, you want to make sure you go down this checklist. Be confident you have calculated correctly:

1. The ministry has been described.

2. The person understands the ministry.

3. Evaluation criteria have been established, and the person knows what is expected.

4. The person has been evaluated over a long enough period of time.

5. The person understands the evaluation (you went over it personally).

6. The ministry cannot be modified to make it possible for the person to function satisfactorily. (This is one of the most common ways to get out of releasing people: tinker with the role and make it fit the person.)

7. Consideration has been given to other ministries in which the person might participate.

8. Adequate notice has been given.

9. Ministry relocation assistance has been offered where appropriate. In other words, getting the person into a different ministry or another location might "save" her for ministry.

10. A termination interview has been held so everyone knows why he is leaving, and follow-up has been conducted after the termination.

Wrap-Up

I leave you in this chapter with the words of Peter Drucker, which I heard in a conference some years ago and paraphrase here: "When I find an employee who is not functioning well, I ask several questions: 'Can the employee do this job?' If the answer is no, obviously I get rid of him. If the answer is yes, I go on to the second question. 'Can he do this job better than any other job?' If the answer is yes, I go on to the third question. 'Can he do this job better than any other job in this organization?' If I get a yes, I go onto the next question. 'Can he do this better than any other job in this organization *under my leadership*?' If that's the problem, then he ought to fire me; but since he can't, I'll do the next best thing and fire him."

Digging Deeper

1. In your own words, explain each word in the list of "Key Words for Biblical Leaders."

2. What are the values of handling evaluation on a personal, "eyeball-to-eyeball" basis?

3. Name at least two types of evaluation you have experienced or used on others. What are the strengths and weaknesses of each type?

4. Which motivational tool do you think would be most effective for your current or future ministry team? Why?

5. Name three things you will do to improve supervision in your ministry over the next year.

Notes

[1] Douglas McGregor, "Theory X: The Traditional View of Direction and Control," in *An Inroduction to School Administration*, ed. M. Chester Nolte (New York: McMillan, 1966), 175.

True Team Decision-Making

*"The lot is cast into the lap, but its every
decision is from the LORD." (Prov. 16:33)*

II

Traditional wisdom tells us that *groups discuss and leaders decide.* I have read almost those exact words in leadership books. We are all familiar with the workings of a president's cabinet: the cabinet officers tell the president what they think; then the president goes into his office and makes the decision. It does not matter if he is the president of the Boy Scouts or the president of the United States.

But recent research at the University of Rhode Island shows that the quality of team decision-making is considerably higher than the quality of individual decision-making. Yes, there are times when you have no choice. There could be privacy or security factors, or maybe the decision must be determined immediately and you cannot call the team together. So the old "80/20" rule comes into the picture. If you demonstrate serious team decision-making 80 percent of the time, the team will not be upset if you have to make 20 percent of the decisions on your own. This is certainly biblical: consider Acts 1, 6, 13, and 15. In each passage God's people practice group decision-making.

Out of all the missionary journeys described in the book of Acts, the apostle Paul was alone and deciding what to do by himself only one time! Paul looks like the dominant figure in Acts. Everyone knows he was the big boss, the head honcho, the big *kahuna.* Yet while writing a commentary on Acts, I was amazed to see something I had not noticed before in my study of Acts. All the missionary activity recorded in that pivotal book was group ministry.

The one exception occurs in Acts 17 where Paul comes to Athens, not to preach but to save his life. He was supposed to sit down, rest up, and wait for the team. But his soul was upset by the idolatry he saw. I am not suggesting Paul was wrong, only that this exception proves the rule that the missionary team worked together. They made group decisions under the leading of the Spirit and sometimes even with God's direct voice, sometimes even through Paul. Team decision-making was the norm in the New Testament.

What Team Leadership Is Not

We have been talking about this from the first chapter, but as it pertains to decision-making, let there be no misunderstanding. Team leadership is not free-rein leadership. It does not encourage individuals to "do their own thing." Nor is it likely to be autocratic. Rather, on a continuum with free rein located all the way to the left and autocracy all the way to the right, there are many options along the way, many blends of leadership style.

Team leadership is not guiding the group to accept the leader's viewpoint. We call that manipulation. Team leadership is not an avoidance of authority and structure. It may appear that way sometimes as a leader glances around the room asking, "What do we do about this? We have to decide today. What do you think? How should we proceed?" And you see heads nodding agreement, smiles on some faces, and there seems to be consensus. People may say, "There is no structure to this. Nobody is following *Robert's Rules of Order*." That is not the point. Team decision-making is not majority rule. I have no problem using *Robert's Rules of Order* if the constitution and bylaws say so. That does not stop us from making group decisions.

Team leadership is not avoidance of a difficult situation, which we commonly call "buck-passing." All of the team agrees together. Keep our motive in mind here. We want to train more and better leaders. We want the team(s) to become more competent and comfortable at leadership. You know they will not do that unless they have responsibilities on their own, unless they have objectives to achieve and know they are part of the decision-making process. Team decision-making is not the absence of formality. Popcorn and Pepsi are not mandatory for group decision-making. You can have a formal situation, very quiet and dignified, and still get the job done.

How to Promote Group Decision-Making

Group decision-making seeks diverse opinions; it does not try to avoid them. Team leaders never say, "I hope Bill will not be at the meeting tonight because I know his viewpoint on this. He will throw all of us out of whack with his different ideas." We *seek* diverse opinions. We will get better decisions if we hear as many sides as we can. We also meet with people one on one. *Leaders should be surprised as rarely as possible.*

One of the first things you teach your volunteers is to tell you anything they know that you might not know but should. That is why you meet with people personally. It explains why coming into a meeting, you already know that Bill has a different viewpoint. You do not try to hold the meeting without him. You do not try to keep him from talking. In fact, you deliberately invite him to talk. Let him make his best case. Let everybody hear it.

Keep your superiors posted. I do this automatically. I currently hold an honorary position as a Scholar-in-Residence, a very informal, non-paid job. I am accountable to no one and do not have to attend any meetings, nor do I have any specific responsibilities. Nevertheless, I prepare an annual Scholar-in-Residence report of five or six pages describing what I have done throughout the year. Nobody ever asks me for that; neither the president nor the board has ever said, "The Scholar-in-Residence must give an annual report." If they had I would have said, "Great! That's what I planned to do anyway." That has been my practice throughout my ministry. I want people to know what I am doing; then if I am doing what they do not wish me to do, they can speak up and get me to change my ways.

Next, *enlist specific rather than broad support in decisions.* Please do not let people sit back, yawn, and say, "Okay, whatever. Fine. Let's do it." You want enthusiastic people who have thought and prayed about decisions and believe collectively they have made the right decision.

Finally, *generate alternative currencies.* (The field of Leadership and Management has it own vocabulary, and this is a good example.) "Alternative" in this context means currencies other than money. For example, friendship, kindness—numerous ways in which you break down barriers that keep people from being part of the group. Joking with a person is not manipulation. Being friendly is not manipulation. Being kind certainly is not manipulation. But such behaviors break down barriers and create alternative currencies so you can make decisions with confidence that you know how the team feels. Resist sitting there and arguing until someone gives up. Such behavior is not ministry, not Spirit-guided, not biblical, and therefore not Christian.

Decision-Making Risks

We need to always ask ourselves what the decision is really about. What is the ultimate issue at stake? Often the reason people give us for making or supporting a decision will not be the real reason or the main reason. We need to recognize the heart and core issues underlying decisions.

Once the issues of a decision are sorted out, we look at the opportunity first and the risk second. If your people always want to gravitate to risk, they will not make good group decision-makers. Remember what I said about long-range planning? People who are always worried about problems will not make good planning team members. In making decisions, we face three kinds of risks.

The one you can afford because it is reversible. In other words, if we try this, we can always change it. It is not life or death or getting married. We just want to rearrange the Wednesday evening schedule of the kid's club ministry. We can always change the schedule back.

The one you cannot afford because it is not reversible. When you hope to build a new church building on ten acres of land someday and you sign your name in ink on the down payment, it is difficult to undo. You could argue that you can always sell the ten acres, but the decision to own the ten acres is not reversible.

The one you cannot afford not to take. There are times as a leader when you will face such a great opportunity that you just have to do it. While I was president of Miami Christian College, there was a three-story apartment building across the street from us that served as a haven for drug-dealing and prostitution. We had to keep people on guard twenty-four hours a day because of that threat across the street.

One day that building came up for sale. I did not want to buy the building. We did not need a three-story apartment building. But we had to control the neighborhood. To eliminate the drug deals, the prostitution, and the gun shots in the middle of the night, we had to own that building. Our board recognized that, and we grabbed it as fast as we could. Sometimes there are risks you cannot afford not to take.

Key questions must be asked in decision-making. First, *is this the right time to make this decision?* Know your team's readiness just as you do in the process of change. Watch them; talk to them; ask them how they like it. So, again we are confronted with a question about prioritizing. Timeliness is very important in decision-making. Sometimes we face a good decision, but now is not the time to move ahead.

Then, *what is the effect of our cost-benefit analysis?* Which costs are worth which benefits? We want the benefits, but can we pay the costs?

Finally, *how can we ease into this decision?* Major decisions often carry implications of what we call "incrementalism"—taking a big decision and breaking it down step by step and phase by phase. People who change the style of worship in a service should learn this. Completely changing the worship style of a service from one week to the next can only lead to upsetting and hurting many people.

Guidelines for Team Decision-Making

We dare not go into decision-making haphazardly. The group clearly defines the type of decisions it will handle, and the rules are clearly spelled out. I offer only a few suggestions for those rules:

1. Each member has one voice.

2. Each member has an absolute responsibility to express his or her opinion.

3. Each member must listen respectfully to all opinions.

4. Each member must detach himself or herself from an idea after it is presented. The ability to suggest an idea and let people attack it and not feel personally hurt shows maturity. Immature people feel an attack on their ideas equals an attack on them.

5. Each member must publicly support the group decision even if he or she does not like it. Group decision-making is not unanimity, but it is an iron-clad commitment to support the team.

6. Each member must keep group processes confidential.

You will see immediately that this process cannot be implemented by immature people. Children, physically or spiritually, cannot do these things. Children talk about what went on inside the group outside the group. They say things like, "They didn't let me talk in the meeting or I would have told them what I thought of their decision." Please grasp the importance of this. Educators stress the importance of "successive rehearsals" for learning. I could not go over this list too often. Read it again. Put it in print and hang it around your neck. Write it on your arm.

Ingredients in the Decision-Making Process

You could easily guess *clarity, accuracy, and timeliness* of information. And please remember you rarely have all the facts. Some leaders say, "I will make the decision when I have all the facts." But really, when do you know you have all the facts? Do you know how many facts there are? Are you counting them so that when fifteen come in you make the decision? Furthermore, whose "facts" do you have? Perhaps Maria and Jason offer differing versions of the events in question. What are the facts? Be careful here.

Look at appropriate approaches, or paradigms, to the decision-making process. For example, you may use a problem-solving grid, a decision tree showing "plan A" and "plan B" optioning, or a chart tracking your flexibility or your openness to change. Changing a bad decision is not a weakness but rather a strength of leadership.

However, as important as they are, decision-making paradigms do not automatically lead you to all the right decisions. That is the Holy Spirit's role.

He uses any tool we can bring to the process. A team without paradigms cannot make decisions as well as a team with paradigms, simply because the latter has more information and the Holy Spirit works through that information.

There are many more ingredients. *Freedom from pressure and publicity* is necessary. I wonder how the president of the United States ever makes a decision with cameras clicking and the press nosing around all the time. We also need *commitment to the effort* of seeking broader insights, responsibility, and accountability. All of this is called the "noetic process," a conscious, voluntary group effort centering on broad viewpoints, geared toward developing new perceptions. That is team decision-making.

Decision-Making Criteria

You can measure whether your decision was a good one by evaluating it in two dimensions: *quality* and *acceptance*. The dimension of quality has to do with effectiveness. A decision is effective if it works. A decision has acceptance if people like it. Acceptance is crucial because even if it works, if the stakeholders do not like it, you may have a problem on your hands. Remember, product and process!

Decision quality can be predicted and measured. Acceptance is less reliably predictable. When your decision-making team looks at something they might or might not do, they can measure the quality of the decision more easily than they can the acceptance of the decision. Therefore, you ought to put forth extra effort in the acceptance. Have small group meetings. Let the team members work with small groups of people from the church or a particular ministry program so you have some idea of the attitudes you face.

Finally, decision quality has to do with the intrinsic value of the decision parameters. The parameters give clues about whether decisions work, how long they work, how well they work, and whether they get us where we want to be with respect to objectives and goals. Decision acceptance gains extrinsic value by group response. You ask, "Which do we want?" We want both. We want quality and we want acceptance. We want to make *good* decisions. We want people to *like* our decisions.

Wrap-Up

Let's just review what we have been talking about so there is no misunderstanding. Group decision-making does not mean that everybody in the organization decides everything. It means that you have a decision-making team—maybe the pastor and the associate staff or elders, maybe a ministry program leader and key volunteers, maybe a committee or a board. A group of people collectively decides something.

Be careful that you teach people how to do this. Do not say, "Okay, people, you are used to me making all of the decisions. We will not do that anymore; we are going to make decisions together." It doesn't happen that way. It happens slowly. People have to be trained; people have to be taught. Steps need to be taken to promote the group decision-making process. Responsibilities and guidelines must be set up. Mainly, people need to know what you are doing and why. I commend this process of team decision-making to you. It is not taught often, but obviously I think it is the way to go. I like it most because I think it is biblical.

Digging Deeper

1. Name other places in the New Testament where you see group decision-making.

2. Why is it important to seek diverse opinions when making decisions? What are practical ways you could do this on a team?

3. Think of a decision your church or ministry program made recently. What was the process and results? What were the opportunities and risks involved?

4. Pick one of the guidelines for team decision-making and explain why it is important. What are additional guidelines you might add to the list?

5. Evaluate a recent decision in terms of quality and acceptance. What could have been done to improve either dimension?

MAKING LEADERS
OUT OF LEARNERS

"If you point these things out to the brothers, you will be a
good minister of Christ Jesus, brought up in the truths of the
faith and of the good teaching that you have followed." (1 Tim. 4:6)

12

Leadership that produces and sustains unity is described in what I consider to be one of the most important paragraphs in the entire Bible, Philippians 2:1–5:

> *If you have any encouragement from being united with Christ, if any comfort from his love, if any fellowship with the Spirit, if any tenderness and compassion, then make my joy complete by being like-minded, having the same love, being one in spirit and purpose. Do nothing out of selfish ambition or vain conceit, but in humility consider others better than yourselves. Each of you should look not only to your own interests, but also to the interests of others. Your attitude should be the same as that of Christ Jesus.*

Those words are followed by the great *kenosis* passage in verses 6–11, which may very well have been an early church hymn. When people come to this chapter, the *kenosis* passage is usually what they emphasize. But I want to focus on these first five verses. Greek scholars tell us the paragraph contains "first class condition verbs"; therefore, rather than translating it *"If* you have any encouragement . . ."* we could well say, *"Since* you have encouragement from being united with Christ, *since* you have comfort from his love . . ."* all the way through. Notice some truths emerging from this passage. *Uniting leadership emphasizes the invisible.* Oh, how we love the visible! The amount of the offering. The attendance at the services. The number of full-time staff. The crowd of kids who come to the youth group. We are so focused on *quantity* it seems impossible for us to see *quality.*

But this passage does not mention quantity at all; it is all about quality, focusing on the invisible—the sovereign presence of God in His church. The central issue of Christian leadership is not organization, as important as that is. We need to know leadership practice, but the central issues are really spiritual. The Scriptures and spiritual thinking on the subject have permeated every chapter of our study. We need a holistic view of ministry that takes us back to Kingdom thinking again. Biblical leaders need a broad view of what God is doing in His world, His church, His ministry, and His people.

I do not know how many church pastoral search committee documents I have looked at during nearly fifty years in Bible college and seminary work. I would guess it has been well over a hundred. I have seen churches that want a strong leader, a mover, a shaker, churches that want a great preacher or a change agent. I do not recall ever seeing the words *meekness* and *humility*. No one says, "Send us somebody who is meek. Send us somebody who is humble."

How Do You Spot a New Leader?

Leaders must be constantly looking for capable people to train, mentor, and to eventually turn over their leadership positions to them. So how do you spot potential for leadership? You look for a lot of things: *Leadership in the past*, if possible. *Capacity to create or catch vision*. He or she doesn't have to be a visionary thinker but has to be able to get on the team and get with the forward motion. *A constructive spirit of discontent*. Leaders challenge the process. A spirit of discontent would be wrong; but a *constructive* spirit of discontent can be useful. *Practical ideas* that really work in the trenches. *Willingness to take responsibility*. We are an irresponsible society. We need to be responsible people, and we certainly need responsible leaders. *A finishing person*. In John 17 Jesus says, "Father, I am ready to come back to heaven because I have finished the work on earth which you have given me to do."

We need *mental toughness*. Sportscasters talk about this all the time. They mean someone who can get beyond the difficulties. A football player with a constant nagging injury who goes out and gives it his best effort game after game is mentally tough. A Bible teacher struggling with throat problems, maybe chronic laryngitis, continues teaching because he is committed. In today's athletic world I cannot think of anyone who displays this better than Brett Farve, the quarterback for the Green Bay Packers. He has been knocked around for years, but every time he comes on the field he gives it everything he has.

Peer respect means that people who know this person trust him or her— other ministry team members, other church members, other youth leaders, or other choir members. *Family respect* is a big factor in 1 Timothy 3 for both elders and deacons. This can apply to other church leaders as well. Churches dare not appoint or elect leaders who do not have the respect of their families. That is a biblical axiom. New leaders also need *a quality that causes people to listen.* Don't you appreciate people of wisdom who can sit through a meeting, listen to other people speak, be quiet, restrain themselves, and then all of a sudden offer about five sentences that include more wisdom than you have heard from everybody else put together? Those are people you need.

Some questions are in order here: *What will this person do to be liked?* As we think about taking on a new team member, we want to know how far she will go. If you are recruiting a volunteer youth leader, will she let students talk during the Bible study so they will like her? Will she shy away from challenging youth to pursue higher standards?

Then we want to know if this person has a *destructive weakness.* Not just a character flaw. We all have character flaws—we are sinners! But does this person have a destructive weakness? One of the destructive weaknesses I watch for in church ministry is anger, or, rather, the inability to control anger. Imagine a church leader who can kick over his chair, shout at other members around the table, grab up his papers, and leave, slamming the door. You know what that proves? He should never have been placed in leadership at all. That is a destructive weakness.

We want to know if this person can *accept reasonable mistakes* or if she is absolutely thrown by every mistake. People make lots of mistakes in ministry. We all do stupid things. Thank God, He is forgiving. Finally, *can we provide this new leader the environment* he needs to succeed? This is the old Peter Drucker question (see the end of chapter 10) about firing again: Can this person work under my leadership?

What Do Leaders Do?

Some years ago George Barna called and asked me to write a chapter in his book *Leaders on Leadership.*[1] He assigned the chapter "What Leaders Do." What did I write?

♦ *Leaders relate.* That is the first thing. Leadership style deals with exactly how you see yourself in relationship to your colleagues—the veracity, the vulnerability, the style, the decentralization that you are willing to demonstrate.

♦ *Leaders are organized.* You may remember that I said earlier that organization may be the cornerstone of leadership and administrative activity. The ministry description comes in here as well as the organizational chart, showing how a leader is involved with other people.

♦ *Leaders achieve.* Leaders relate, organize, and achieve through goal setting, planning, and setting priorities. The small wins are just as important as the big ones.

♦ *Leaders think.* You would not commonly see this in leadership books, because at times leaders seem too busy to think. *Good leaders think.* Critical thinking, effective decision-making, and cooperation with other people all fit in here. Good leaders arrange their lives so that they have thinking time. They do not *hope* they have thinking time. They do not *dismiss the idea* by saying that they would have thinking time if they were not so busy. They must come to the conclusion that they are not the best leaders they could be if they do not have verifiable thinking time.

♦ *Leaders envision.* They view the uniqueness of the organization, the vision, and the time it would take to get there. Vision should emphasize the long term. Yes, God sometimes changes our plans and prevents us from seeing a vision reach its fulfillment. Yes, the man from Macedonia appeared to Paul and said, "Don't go north, come west" (Acts 16:9). This was God's leading. But paying the price of patience is one way leaders stay in place. Long-held ministry positions are desirable. Long leadership roles are commended. We do not need people who change leadership roles every few months. When I see that on a former student's résumé, I stop writing letters of recommendation. I am not interested in helping people jump from place to place for whatever reason, though sometimes there are good reasons for moving.

♦ *Leaders endure.* They relate, they organize, they achieve, they think, they envision, and they endure. Success does not breed success. Failure, if properly utilized, breeds success!

♦ *Leaders learn to fail and bounce back and to lean on their call.* Good leaders know that God called them to a particular ministry, and therefore they stay through the problems. The one thing that sustains them in those hours of anguish is an awareness of God's call.

Do You Think You Are Irreplaceable?

Here are some signs to identify whether that could be the case. You may think you are irreplaceable if you *find yourself delegating reluctantly and with complete direction.* You always seem to have more work than your volunteers or staff members do. You never take a vacation, only a day or two at a time, and you rue those. When you are away, your supervisor has to put out the fires and take care of all the problems that your absence created.

You may think you are irreplaceable *if your team members' skills have been static over the last year.* Or if you experience a lot of turnover. Team members rarely come to you with ideas because nothing would be done with their ideas. *No one can fill in when you are gone, and subordinates do not seem promotable.* In other words, you have created a cocoon around yourself so that nobody else can do what you do in the way you do it; nobody else knows how to do it. Nobody else knows anything about it because you have not told them.

What Are the Marks of a Workaholic?

These are so convicting I almost don't want to deal with them. What are the marks of a workaholic?

◆ *Inability to accept failure.* We need what my friend Vernon Grounds called in an article in *Christianity Today* "the faith to face failure."[2]

◆ *Incessant work patterns.* Late hours. Carrying your work home. No time off.

◆ *Guilt over low productivity.* Concern at the end of each day that you haven't done enough—the hours are just eaten up.

◆ *Anxiety or depression.* So many people in our day deal with this. But it is hardly a new problem. Consider Elijah in 1 Kings 19 or Job in Job chapter 3.

◆ *Subjective standards of success.* Just going along with the world's idea of success rather than looking biblically at ministerial effectiveness.

◆ *Leisure time guilt.* I love a Reuel Howe quote in an old book where he claims maturity is the ability to work without playing and to play without thinking you ought to be working.

◆ *Self-denial* sounds good at first, but here we are talking about being ruled by the clock even to the point of health failure.

◆ *Future orientation.* So dissatisfied with the present that you cannot stand it and are constantly impatient.

Quite frankly, I have suffered all of these through my leadership years at one time or another. I know they are very real. Here are some practical suggestions on defeating workaholism:

- See people and respond to them as people.

- Give of yourself, not just things.

- Enhance your sensory awareness.

- Develop a capacity for spontaneity. (I am not very good at that, but I work at it.)

- Make yourself slow down. (I don't know if I will ever do that. Maybe in heaven.)

- Find a pleasant avocation or hobby. (Finally I win one. Give me a tennis racquet and I am ready to put aside my work for a while.)

- Forgive yourself. God forgives you. Other people will forgive you. You need to forgive yourself for failings in all these things.

- Keep your balance on the ministry-leadership ladder. (See below.)

Wrap-Up

Let's close with a diagram that helps us to visualize the last point above. All the rungs are not only real, but self-explanatory. Grab hold tightly! You need that top rung.

MEDITATION

MINISTRY

TASK

NEED

REALITY

EXPECTATION

INSTRUCTION:

KEEPING YOUR BALANCE ON THE LEADERSHIP LADDER

Digging Deeper

1. Explain the main points of Philippians 2:1–5 as if you were giving a leadership devotional talk for your next team meeting.

2. To say we should be "spotting new leaders" is one thing, but in your specific situation, how do you go about that?

3. Memorize and be able to explain the six things leaders do.

4. Analyze yourself for signs of workaholism. What might you do to attack this problem?

5. Explain the ladder diagram. What does it teach you about leadership?

Notes

[1] Kenneth O. Gangel, "What Leaders Do," in *Leaders on Leadership*, ed. George Barna (Ventura, Calif.: Regal, 1997), 31–46.

[2] Vernon C. Grounds, "Faith to Face Failure," *Christianity Today* (December 9, 1977), 13.

BIBLIOGRAPHY

Anderson, Leith. *Leadership That Works*. Minneapolis, Minn.: Bethany House, 1999.

Anthony, Michael J. *The Effective Church Board*. Grand Rapids, Mich.: Baker Book House, 1993.

Barna, George. *Leaders on Leadership*. Ventura, Calif.: Regal Books, 1997.

Berkley, James D., ed. *Leadership and Administration*. Vol. 3 of *Leadership Handbooks of Practical Theology*. Grand Rapids, Mich.: Baker Books, 1994.

Cedar, Paul. *Strength in Servant Leadership*. Waco, Tex.: Word, 1987.

Clark, Kenneth E., and Miriam B. Clark. *Choosing to Lead*. Charlotte, N.C.: Leadership Press, 1994.

De Pree, Max. *Leading Without Power*. San Francisco: Jossey-Bass, 1997.

Finzel, Hans. *Empowered Leaders*. Nashville, Tenn.: Word, 1998.

Gangel, Kenneth O., and Samuel L. Canine. *Communication and Conflict Management in Churches and Christian Organizations*. Nashville, Tenn.: Broadman, 1993.

Gangel, Kenneth O. *Coaching Ministry Teams*. Nashville, Tenn.: Word, 1999.

Gangel, Kenneth O. *Feeding and Leading*. Wheaton, Ill.: Victor Books, 1989.

Gangel, Kenneth O. *Team Leadership in Christian Ministry*. Chicago, Ill.: Moody Press, 1997.

Habecker, Eugene. *Rediscovering the Soul of Leadership*. Wheaton, Ill.: Victor Books, 1996.

Habecker, Eugene. *The Other Side of Leadership*. San Francisco: Jossey-Bass, 1992.

Hesselbein, Francis, Marshall Goldsmith, and Richard Beckhard, eds. *The Leader of the Future*. San Francisco: Jossey-Bass, 1996.

Kotter, John P. *How Leadership Differs From Management*. New York: Free Press, 1990.

Kouzes, James M., and Barry Z. Posner. *Encouraging the Heart*. San Francisco: Jossey-Bass, 1999.

Kouzes, James M., and Barry Z. Posner. *The Leadership Challenge*. Rev. ed. San Francisco: Jossey-Bass, 1995.

Kouzes, James M., and Barry Z. Posner. *The Leadership Challenge Planner*. San Francisco: Jossey-Bass, 1999.

Means, James E. *Leadership in Christian Ministry*. Grand Rapids, Mich.: Baker Book House, 1989.

Nanus, Burt. *Visionary Leadership*. San Francisco: Jossey-Bass, 1992.

Roberts, Randall. *Lessons in Leadership*. Grand Rapids, Mich.: Kregel, 1999.

Strauch, Alexander. *Biblical Eldership*. Littleton, Colo.: Lewis and Roth Publishers, 1995.

Williams, Dennis, and Kenneth O. Gangel. *Volunteers for Today's Church*. Grand Rapids, Mich.: Baker Book House, 1993. Reprint, Eugene, Oreg.: Wipf and Stock, 2004.

Wilkes, C. Gene. *Jesus on Leadership*. Wheaton, Ill.: Tyndale House, 1998.

NOTES

NOTES

NOTES

NOTES